Performance Notes by Bob Gulla and Frank Martyn

ISBN: 978-1-4234-4038-3

CORPORATION

7777 W. BLUEMOUND RD. P.O. BOX 13819 MILWAUKEE, WI 53213

Visit Hal Leonard Online at
www.halleonard.com

Table of Contents

Introduction

· ·

Welcome to *Movie Piano Songs For Dummies!* In this wonderful collection I show you how to play many of the finest movie songs and themes. Discover the work of some of the greatest songwriters and film composers of our time, from Burt Bacharach and John Barrie to The Beatles. Learn and love the gorgeous music from super epic films like *Exodus* and *Spartacus* to more humorous and fun-loving fare like The Beatles' *A Hard Day's Night* and Disney's *The Jungle Book.* All of the songs here have two common elements. The first is pure and simple greatness. They are enduring works by legendary composers. The second is that these compositions invariably enhance the films they underscore. John Williams' "Theme from Jurassic Park," and "Moon River," Mancini's classic from *Breakfast at Tiffany's,* make the pictures they appear in more enjoyable. Some of these songs, like Marvin Hamlisch's "The Way We Were" have even taken on lives of their own, and have become bigger than their blockbuster films.

Along with great performances, a good script, magnificent cinematography, and adroit direction, expert film scores contribute mightily to the overall success of a motion picture. When the marriage of movie and music is just right, it creates a transcendent experience.

The songs in this compendium are suitable for a wide range of abilities, from beginners to more experienced players. Explore the pages of these performance notes, walk up and down the aisles of our virtual nickelodeon, and find the many songs that will undoubtedly fit your taste and expertise. Then you too will appreciate how music and movies combine to create one of entertainment's most magical thrills!

About This Book

For every song here, I include a little background or history. Sometimes I discuss the artist, the song, the movie, or some other interesting element of the song. This information is followed by a variety of tidbits that struck me as I made my way through the teaching of these songs, including some of the following:

✔ A run-down of the parts you need to know.

✔ A breakdown of some of the chord progressions important to playing the song effectively.

✔ Some of the critical information you need to navigate the sheet music.

✔ Some tips and shortcuts you can use to expedite the learning process.

In many cases, you may already know how to do a lot of this. If so, feel free to skip over those familiar bits.

How to Use This Book

The music in this book is in standard piano notation — a staff for the melody and lyrics above the traditional piano grand staff. I assume you know a little something about reading music, and that you know a little bit about playing piano — such as how to hold your fingers, basic chords, and how to look cool while doing it. If you need a refresher course on piano, please check out *Piano For Dummies* by Blake Neely (Wiley).

I recommend that you first play through the song, and then practice all the main sections and chords. From there, you can add the tricks and treats of each one — and there are many. Approach the song one section at a time and then assemble them together in a sequence. This technique helps to provide you with a greater understanding of how the song is structured, and enables you to play it through more quickly.

In order to follow the music and my performance notes, you need a basic understanding of scales and chords. But if you're not a wiz, don't worry. Just spend a little time with the nifty tome *Music Theory For Dummies* by Michael Pilhofer and Holly Day (Wiley), and with a little practice, you'll be on your way to entertaining family and friends.

Glossary

As you might expect, I use quite a few musical terms in this book. Some of these may be unfamiliar to you, so here are a few right off the bat that can help your understanding of basic playing principles:

- ✔ **Arpeggio:** Playing the notes of a chord one at a time rather than all together
- ✔ **Bridge:** Part of the song that is different from the verse and the chorus, providing variety and connecting the other parts of the song to each other
- ✔ **Coda:** The section at the end of a song, which is sometimes labeled with the word "coda"
- ✔ **Chorus:** The part of the song that is the same each time through, usually the most familiar section
- ✔ **Hook:** A familiar, accessible, or singalong melody, lick, or other section of the song
- ✔ **Verse:** The part of the song that tells the story; each verse has different lyrics, and each song generally has between two and four of these

Icons Used in This Book

In the margins of this book are lots of little icons that will help make your life easier:

A reason to stop and review advice that can prevent personal injury to your fingers, your brain, or your ego.

These are optional parts, or alternate approaches that those who'd like to find their way through the song with a distinctive flair can take. Often these are slightly more challenging routes, but encouraged nonetheless, because there's nothing like a good challenge!

This is where you will find notes about specific musical concepts that are relevant but confusing to non-musical types — stuff that you wouldn't bring up, say, at a frat party or at your kid's soccer game.

You get lots of these tips, because the more playing suggestions I can offer, the better you'll play. And isn't that what it's all about?

Alfie

from the Paramount Picture ALFIE
Words by Hal David
Music by Burt Bacharach

Very slowly, rubato

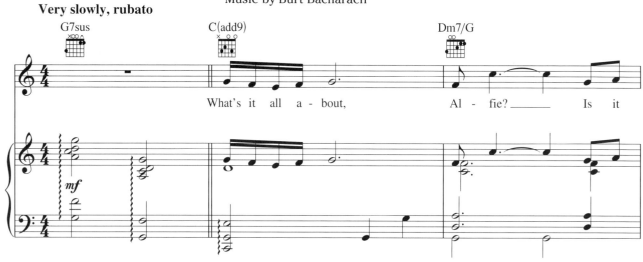

What's it all a - bout, Al - fie? _____ Is it

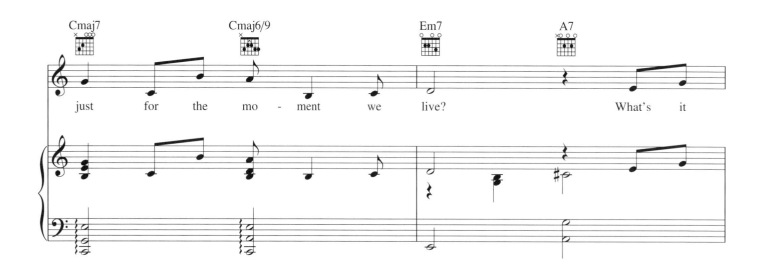

just for the mo - ment we live? What's it

all a - bout _____ when you sort it out, _____ Al - fie? _____

Baby Elephant Walk

from the Paramount Picture HATARI!
Words by Hal David
Music by Henry Mancini

Moderately slow and steady

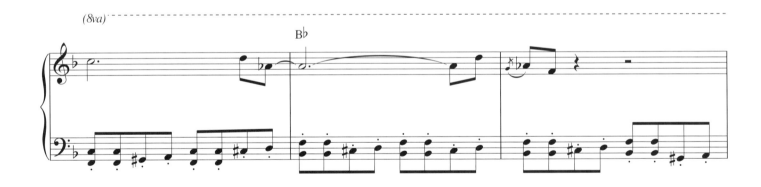

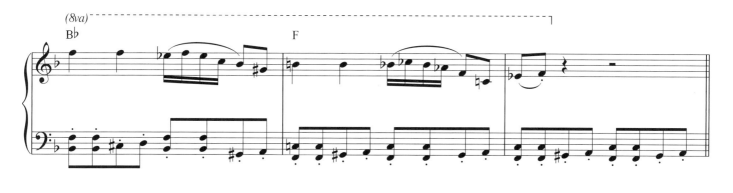

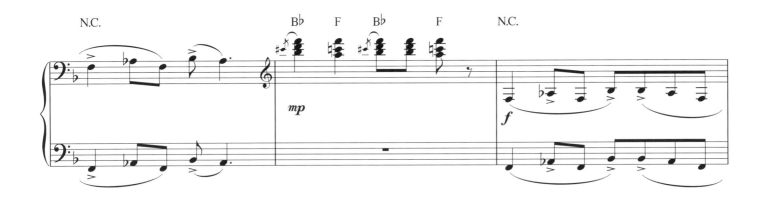

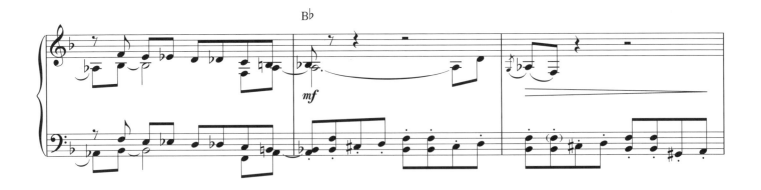

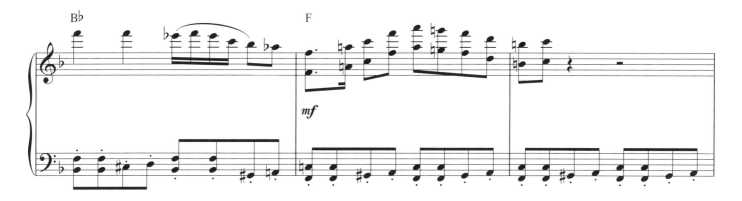

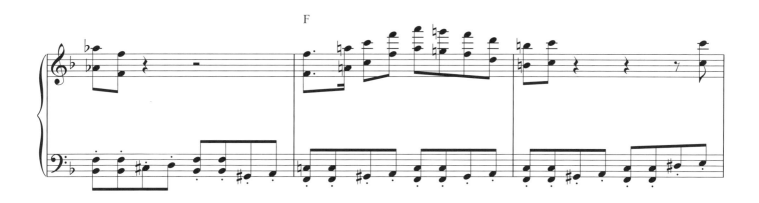

The Bare Necessities

from Walt Disney's THE JUNGLE BOOK
Words and Music by Terry Gilkyson

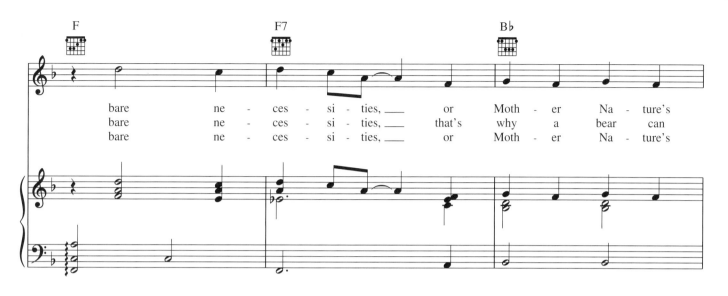

bare ne - ces - si - ties, ___ or Moth - er Na - ture's
bare ne - ces - si - ties, ___ that's why a bear can
bare ne - ces - si - ties, ___ or Moth - er Na - ture's

re - ci - pes ___ that bring the bare ne - ces - si - ties ___ of
rest at ease ___ with just the bare ne - ces - si - ties ___ of
re - ci - pes ___ that bring the bare ne - ces - si - ties ___ of

life. _____ Wher - ev - er I wan - der, _____
life. _____ When you ___ pick a paw - paw _____
life. _____ So just try to re - lax   *Spoken: Oh Yeah!*

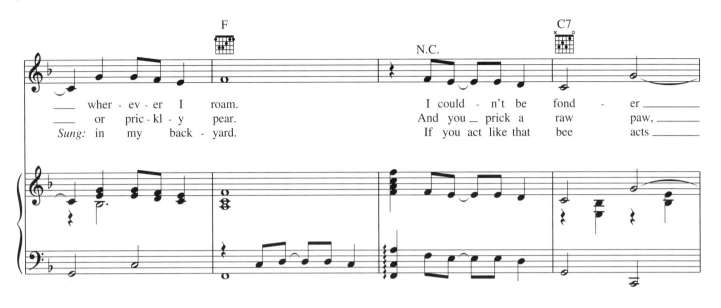

_____ wher - ev - er I roam.
_____ or pric - kl - y pear.
Sung: in my back - yard.

I could - n't be fond - er _____
And you _ prick a raw paw, _____
If you act like that bee acts _____

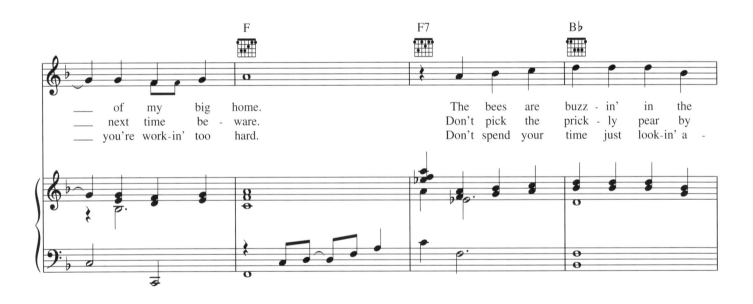

_____ of my big home.
_____ next time be - ware.
_____ you're work - in' too hard.

The bees are buzz - in' in the
Don't pick the prick - ly pear by
Don't spend your time just look - in' a -

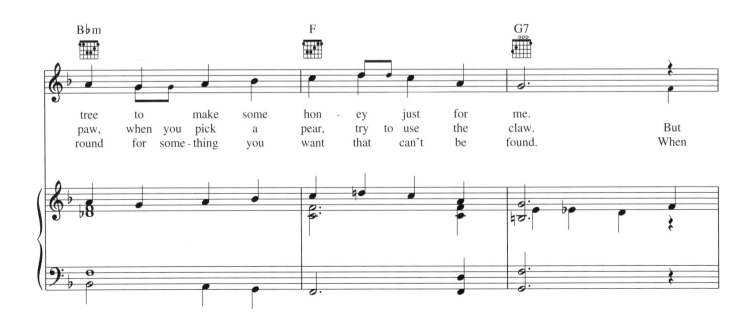

tree to make some hon - ey just for me.
paw, when you pick a pear, try to use the claw.
round for some - thing you want that can't be found.

But
When

Beauty And The Beast

from Walt Disney's BEAUTY AND THE BEAST
Lyrics by Howard Ashman
Music by Alan Menken

Born Free

from the Columbia Pictures' Release BORN FREE
Words by Don Black
Music by John Barry

Candle On The Water

from Walt Disney's PETE'S DRAGON
Words and Music by Al Kasha and Joel Hirschhorn

Edelweiss

from THE SOUND OF MUSIC
Lyrics by Oscar Hammerstein II
Music by Richard Rodgers

The Candy Man

from WILLY WONKA AND THE CHOCOLATE FACTORY
Words and Music by Leslie Bricusse and Anthony Newley

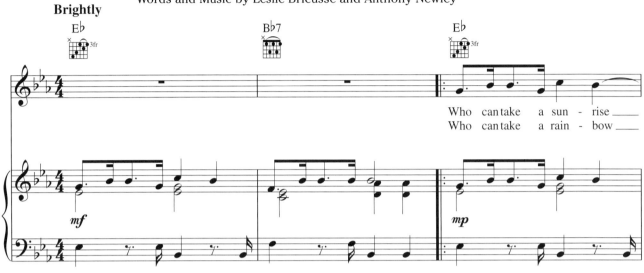

Who can take a sun - rise _____
Who can take a rain - bow _____

sprin - kle it with dew, _____
wrap it in a sigh, _____

cov - er it in choc - 'late and a mir - a - cle or two?}
soak it in the sun and make a straw - b'ry lem - on pie?}

The

Endless Love

from ENDLESS LOVE
Words and Music by Lionel Richie

The Exodus Song

from EXODUS
Words by Pat Boone
Music by Ernest Gold

see a land where chil - dren can run free.   So

take my hand and walk this land with me, and walk this { love - ly } { gold - en } land with

me. Though I am just a man,____ when you are by my side, with the

Ghost

Theme from the Paramount Motion Picture GHOST
By Maurice Jarre

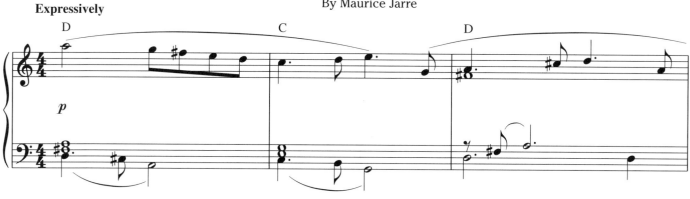

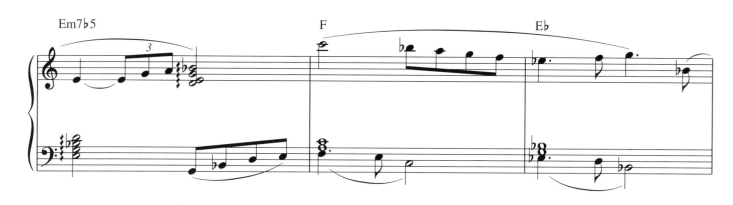

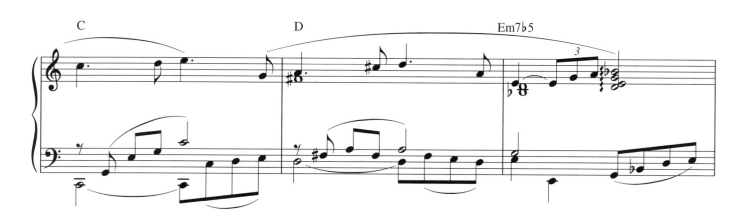

Forrest Gump - Main Title (Feather Theme)

from the Paramount Motion Picture FORREST GUMP
Music by Alan Silvestri

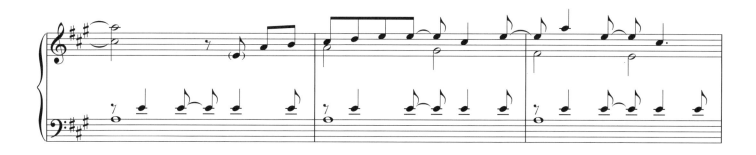

(lightly)

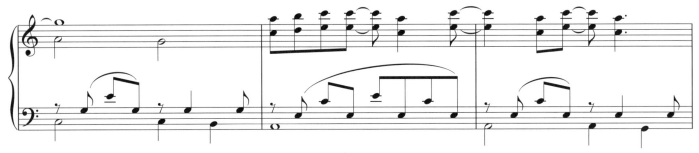

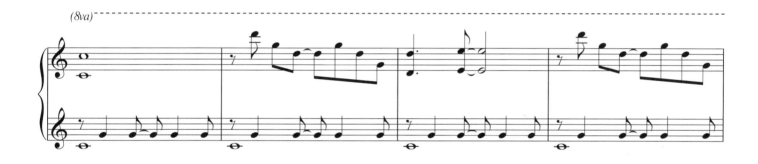

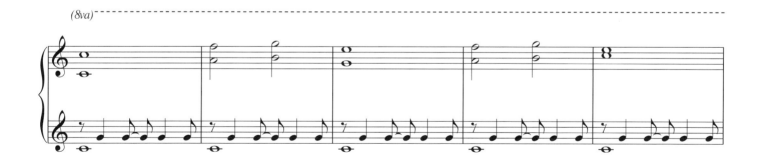

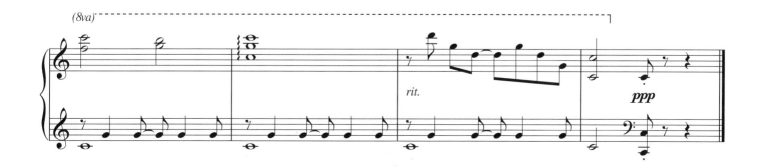

Georgia On My Mind

from RAY
Words by Stuart Gorrell
Music by Hoagy Carmichael

A Hard Day's Night

from A HARD DAY'S NIGHT
Words and Music by John Lennon and Paul McCartney

Moderately, with a beat

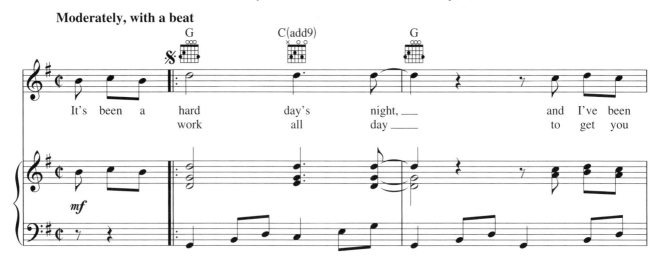

I Am A Man Of Constant Sorrow

featured in O BROTHER, WHERE ART THOU?
Words and Music by Carter Stanley

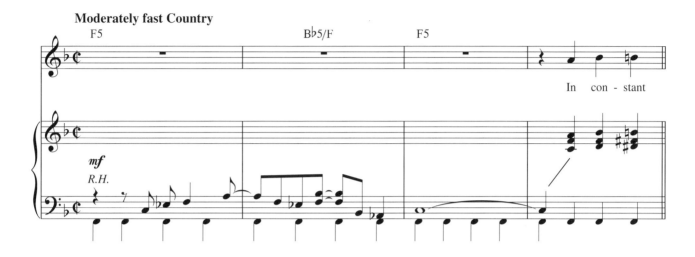

sor - row. _____ I've seen trou - ble all __ my
trou - ble, _____ no pleas - ure here _____ on earth __ I've
lov - er, _____ I nev - er ex - pect _____ to see __ you a -
val - ley _____ for man - y years _____ where I __ may lay,
stran - ger; _____ my face __ you nev - _____ er will see __ no

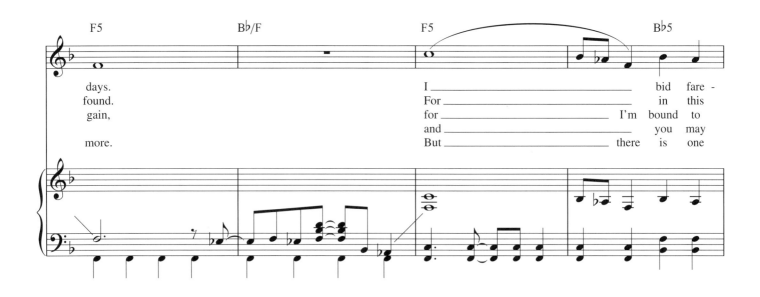

days. _____ I _____ bid fare -
found. _____ For _____ in this
gain, _____ for _____ I'm bound to
and _____ you may
more. _____ But _____ there is one

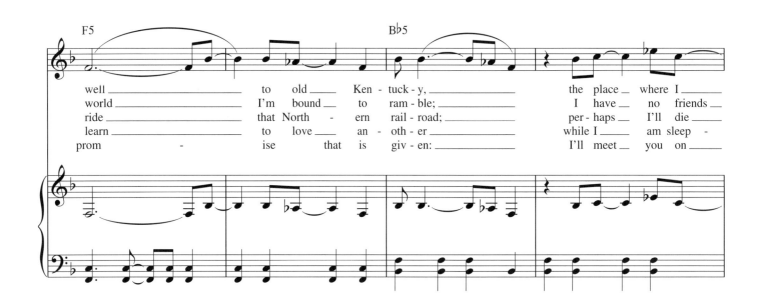

well _____ to old _____ Ken - tuck - y, _____ the place __ where I _____
world _____ I'm bound to ram - ble; _____ I have __ no friends __
ride _____ that North - ern rail - road; _____ per - haps __ I'll die __
learn _____ to love ____ an - oth - er _____ while I _____ am sleep -
prom - _____ ise that is giv - en: _____ I'll meet __ you on _____

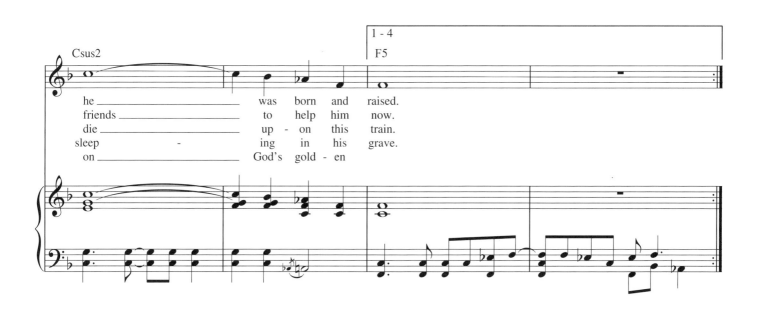

I Will Always Love You

from THE BODYGUARD
Words and Music by Dolly Parton

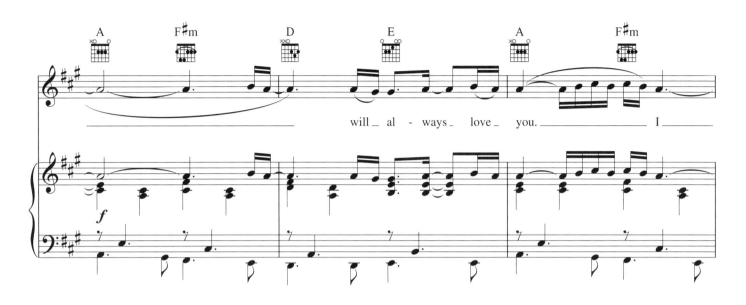

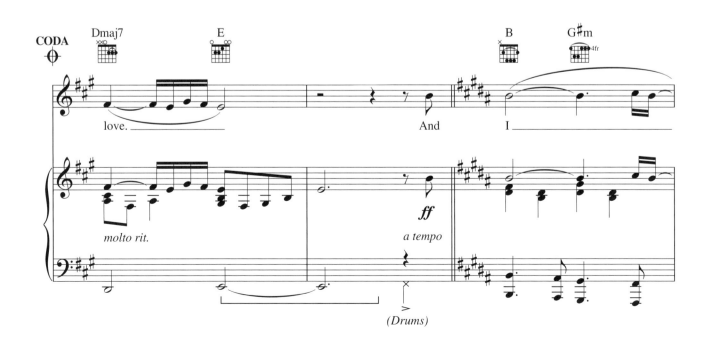

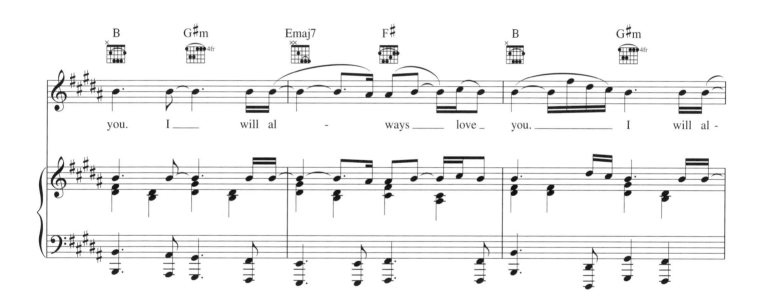

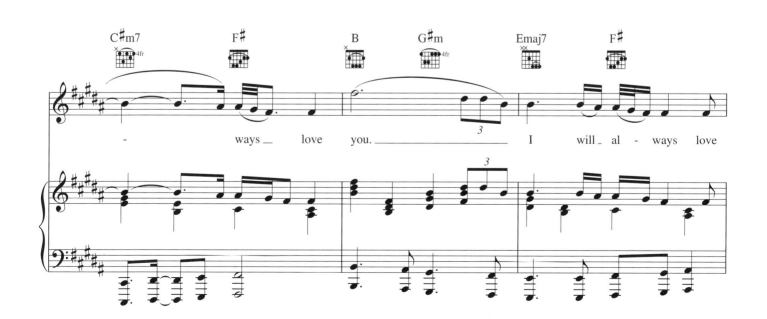

Additional Lyrics

3. I hope life treats you kind.
   And I hope you have all you've dreamed of.
   And I wish to you, joy and happiness.
   But above all this, I wish you love.

Legends Of The Fall

from TriStar Pictures' LEGENDS OF THE FALL
Composed by James Horner

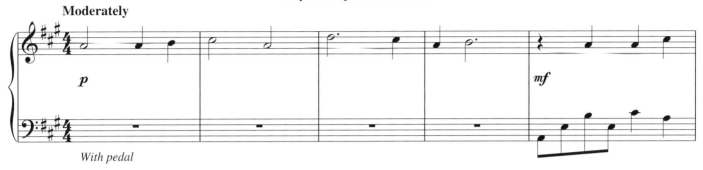

rit.   _a tempo_

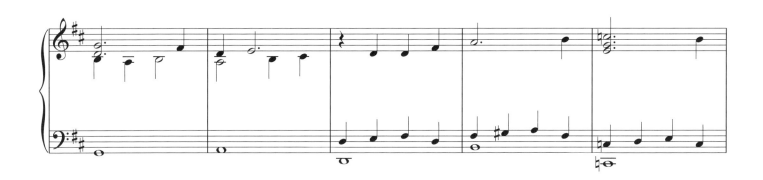

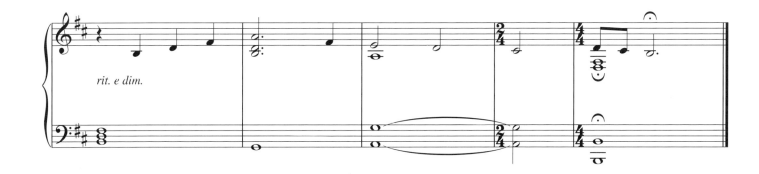

rit. e dim.

Il Postino (The Postman)

from IL POSTINO
Music by Luis Bacalov

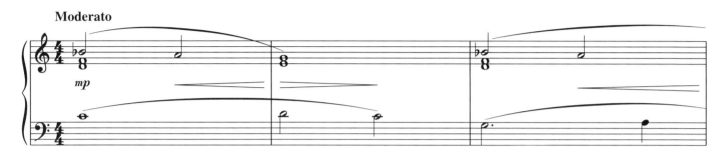

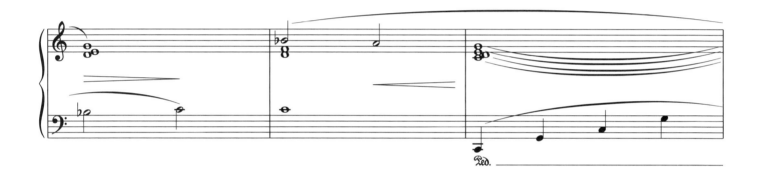

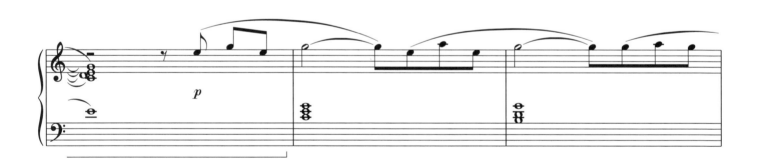

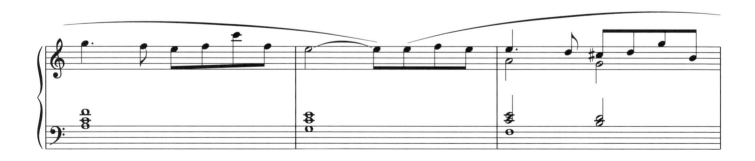

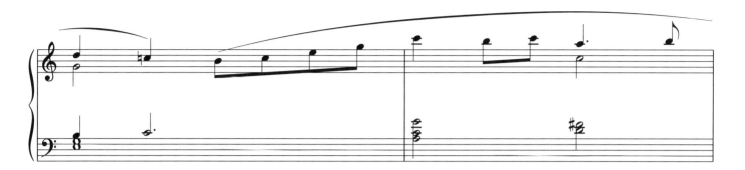
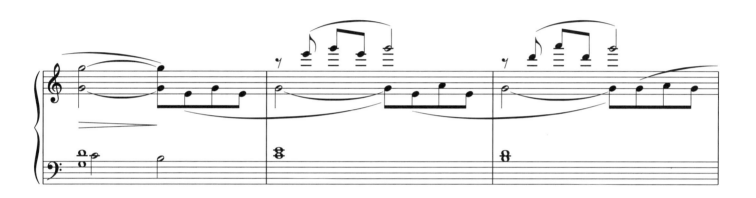

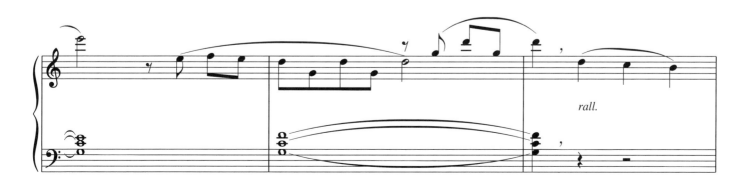

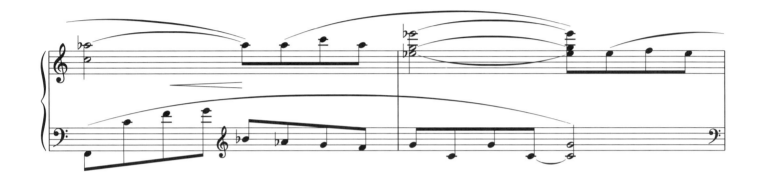

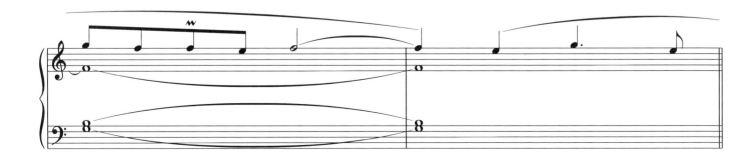

The John Dunbar Theme

from DANCES WITH WOLVES
By John Barry

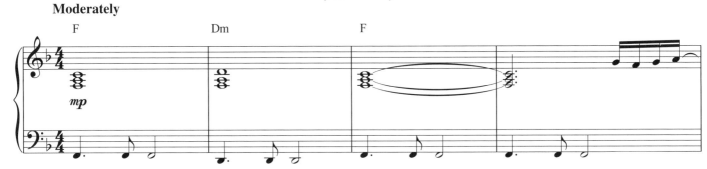

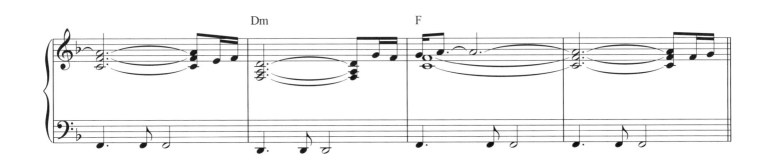

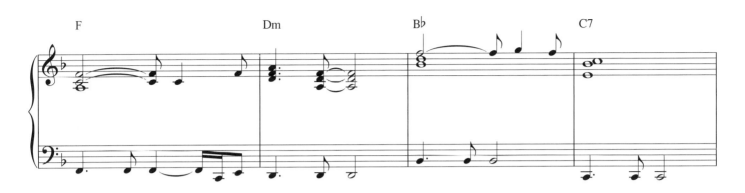

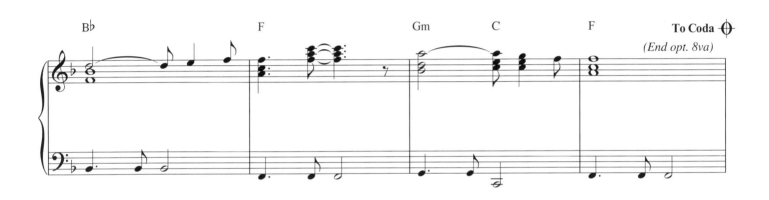

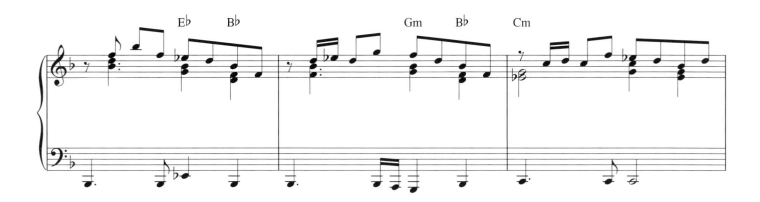

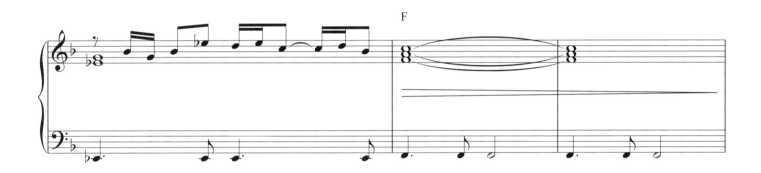

Theme From "Jurassic Park"

from the Universal Motion Picture JURASSIC PARK
Composed by John Williams

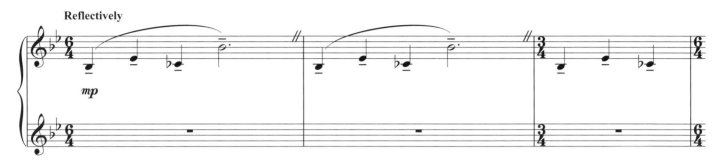

A Man And A Woman (Un Homme Et Une Femme)

from A MAN AND A WOMAN
Original Words by Pierre Barouh
English Words by Jerry Keller
Music by Francis Lai

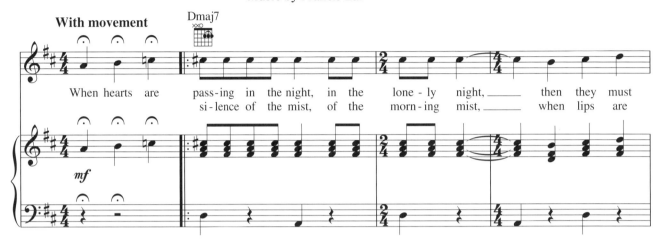

When hearts are pass-ing in the night, in the lone-ly night, _____ then they must
si-lence of the mist, of the morn-ing mist, _____ when lips are

hold each oth-er tight, oh, so ver-y tight _____ and take a chance that in the light, in to-
wait-ing to be kissed, long-ing to be kissed, _____ where is the rea-son to re-sist and de-

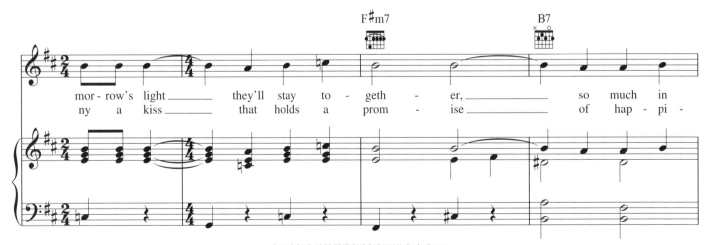

mor-row's light _____ they'll stay to-geth-er, _____ so much in
ny a kiss _____ that holds a prom-ise _____ of hap-pi-

Performance Notes

Alfie (page 6)

"Alfie" is one of the songs Burt Bacharach says he's proudest of. Coming from the man who's written a hundred classics in the pop music canon, this is no small praise. The definitive performance of the song, recorded in 1966, comes from Dionne Warwick, Burt's very favorite vocalist. A more recent rendition comes from British soul singer Joss Stone, with the help of Mick Jagger.

Alfie, the movie Bacharach and lyricist Hal David composed the song for, features Michael Caine (reprised in 2004 by Jude Law) in the title role of a swingin' '60s adventurer. The flick details the womanizing escapades of Alfie, who charms the women and his audience (which he addresses directly) in equal measure. But thanks to a great performance from Caine, it's much more than just a light-hearted romp. It veers unpredictably from pathos to humor, with wide pendulum-like swings of emotion. *Alfie* won a Golden Globe® for Best English Language Foreign Film and a Special Jury Prize at Cannes, while Vivien Merchant, a co-star, received a British award for Most Promising Newcomer. In addition, the film was nominated for five Oscars®.

Make that melody sing! Like a fool in love, this melody leaps and bounds, so play through it once or twice, all by itself. Then, add in the rest and let it dip and soar to its heart's content!

Only fools would rush these fun melodies and lush harmonies. Note the tempo marking: very slowly and *rubato*. *Rubato* means you can slow down or speed up, but just a little. Burt Bacharach's music is full of feeling. So, like the great one, express yourself!

How did Bacharach make "Alfie" sound so rich? By *extending* (or adding onto) basic chords. For example, play the three-note chord (or triad) built on C. C, E, and G (1, 3, and 5) make a C chord. Now, count up two notes and add the B. That is a Cmaj7 chord. Keep counting and adding: C9, C11, and C13. That's how it's done. You've just learned the secret of jazz!

Baby Elephant Walk (page 10)

Mancini wrote "Baby Elephant Walk" in 1961 for the film *Hatari!*, shown in theaters in 1962. The piece was initially intended as a brief excerpt of incidental music to go with a scene where, you guessed it, a baby elephant is taken for a walk. But once audiences heard the playful ditty, the simple tune blossomed into an international hit, and has been recorded by hundreds of artists in many different styles. In the original recording, Mancini uses a playful combination of tuba and woodwinds to convey a sense of an oversized toddler. It's catchy, sure. But its simplicity has made it one of Mancini's most memorable tunes.

Also memorable is the film for which the song was written. *Hatari!*, which means "danger!" in Swahili, follows a group of trappers in Africa dispatched to snag wild animals and sell them to zoos and circuses. The film, starring John Wayne and directed by Howard Hawks, is loose; it began with virtually no script, and the chase and capture sequences almost all involve the real actors pursuing wild, not trained, animals. Rumor has it that Wayne shot a real elephant with the magnum rifle he totes around in the film.

Slide, but don't fall, off this elephant ride. The most common way to play the left-hand pattern is this: Slide your third finger from G♯ to A. Continue using that slide motion, even when the pattern moves! That's called boogie-woogie piano.

Note the *8va* marking above the music. It means you play that part one octave higher. Playing an octave higher is easy. Following the F scale, count up eight notes, now do your fancy finger work.

Watch for *R.H.*, which means right hand. This means, even though all notes are in one staff, the right hand plays the top notes!

Playing boogie-woogie piano is so much fun, you might speed up. The tempo is marked moderately slow and steady. If you have a metronome handy, test your speed. Otherwise, tap your left foot to help keep a steady tempo. That's what it's there for.

The Bare Necessities *(page 14)*

Terry Gilkyson wrote both the words and the music to this entertaining jungle romp, sung by the characters of Baloo and Mowgli in Disney's 1967 hit, *The Jungle Book*. Incidentally, the voice of Mowgli came from Bruce Reitherman, the son of the film's director, Wolfgang Reitherman. The song earned an Academy Award® nomination but lost out to another beastly track: "Talk to the Animals" from the film *Doctor Doolittle*.

Hamilton H. "Terry" Gilkyson III had an astonishing and influential folk music career that, unfortunately, earned little notice from the public. Johnny Cash, the Kingston Trio, Burl Ives, Harry Connick, Jr., Louis Armstrong, Mitch Miller, The Brothers Four, Tony Bennett, Harry Belafonte, The New Christy Minstrels, and hundreds of others recorded his compositions. Phew!

He wrote and recorded "The Cry of the Wild Goose," which Frankie Laine covered for a #1 hit in 1950, as well as the 1953 Top 10 hit "Tell Me a Story," recorded by Laine and Jimmy Boyd. As a singer-songwriter Gilkyson co-wrote "On Top of Old Smoky" with the Weavers, a Top 10 hit in 1951. With his performing group The Easy Riders, he co-wrote the 1953 Top 10 hit "Mister Tap Toe" recorded by Doris Day. Gilkyson and The Easy Riders scored their own hit with the self-written "Marianne," and they teamed with Laine again on the smash "Love Is a Golden Ring." In the '60s he left the group to take a job with Disney, writing music for the television show, "The Wonderful World of Disney," and the studio's movies.

Make a little noise in this boisterous jaunt! Marked loud (*f*) from the first measure, the party never stops. Keep the dynamics steady throughout, roaring above the din of the jungle.

Don't let your paws drag on this brightly bouncing ditty. In *cut time*, (2/2, marked by a C with a slash through it), each measure has two nicely accented beats. So, feel this as "one, two, one, two . . . ," a favorite among dancing bears.

Welcome to the jungle of rolled chords. The very first notes of the song are *rolled* (marked by the wavy line). Play the notes, from bottom to top, quickly yet smoothly. This skill will be valuable . . . that same chord is lurking other places in the song.

Short, quick pedaling works best for this type of safari. The *sustain pedal* (the far right one) is helpful to keep those notes ringing, but holding the pedal down too long makes notes blur. As tones change, don't be a lead foot! When in doubt, just listen and let your ear guide you!

Beauty and the Beast (page 18)

Alan Menken, who wrote this tune with lyricist Howard Ashman, has been on one heck of a hot streak. Originally a jingle composer, nightclub performer, and later, a musical theatrical songwriter, Menken made the jump to Hollywood in the late '80s, and since then has become legendary. His brilliant compositions for Disney films are virtually unparalleled, with hits from *Pocahontas* ("Colors of the Wind"), *Aladdin* ("A Whole New World"), *The Little Mermaid* ("Part of Your World"), *The Hunchback of Notre Dame*, and so on. Menken's musical compositions are as much a part of the legendary Disney film canon as the animation and characters themselves. His work for *Beauty and the Beast* may be the House of Mouse's best marriage of music and movie, with many memorable musical moments.

In fact, *Beauty and the Beast* ranks #22 on the American Film Institute's list of Best Musicals and #34 on its list of Best Romantic American Movies, and Menken's composition ranks #62 on the list of the Greatest Songs from American Movies. That track especially, performed by Celine Dion and Peabo Bryson, and again by Angela Lansbury (as the voice of Mrs. Potts) caps the film beautifully at both ends.

So beautifully, that the movie won Oscars® in 1991 for Best Original Score and Best Original Song. The film itself is the only animated picture ever to be nominated in the Best Picture category. Menken is no stranger to awards. While his "Beauty" earned many prizes, he's been bestowed an embarrassment of GRAMMY® and Oscar riches.

Be smooth to win this beauty. *Lyrically* means to make the melody sing. Use the *sustain pedal* (the far right one) for each sung phrase. Push it down when the melody starts and let up when it stops. You'll hear it when it's right. So just play it by ear!

In every love story, someone changes the key! This song changes from E♭ to F halfway through. Three flats become one flat. And it becomes loud there. The *f*, or *forte*, means you don't have to be sneaky about it.

Make your piano a singer. Find the melody note in the right hand chord (it's usually the top note, but not always) and make it a little bit louder. That's called *voicing*.

Play with feeling. Speed and loudness (tempo and dynamics) change throughout this tune. So, keep a keen eye out for those markings.

Born Free (page 22)

Sometime in the mid '50s, Joy Adamson, wife of George Adamson, the game warden of the Northern Frontier District in Kenya, watched as her husband shot and fatally killed a lioness, which was charging him to protect her three cubs. The Adamsons took the cubs, Elsa, Lustica, and Big One, home to raise. Joy wrote her book, *Born Free*, to describe the unusual nurturing that went into raising the cubs, especially Elsa, the cub that she kept the longest. The book became an international best-seller, was printed in several different languages, and, in 1966, was turned into an Academy Award-winning movie of the same name.

John Barry's score of the film, which won one of those Oscars, proved to be a highlight. The title tune became a hit for its singer, the sonorously voiced Matt Monro. An instrumental version by pianist Roger Williams also hit the Top 10 in the summer of 1966, and a version by a Cleveland soul group called The Hesitations cracked the Top 40 in January of 1968. Andy Williams, another singer with a creamy voice, kept the tune popular through the '70s with his rendition and album of the same name. For his part, composer Barry was on his way to becoming one of the most celebrated film composers of all time, winning five Academy Awards and four Grammys. Barry first made a name for himself scoring James Bond film soundtracks, of which he wrote at least a dozen. His style features sweeping, lyrical themes and deftly appointed orchestration. He draws from a wide range of influences, including pop, classical, jazz, and big band sounds. Barry, born in York in northern England, was predestined to be a film composer. His mother was a classical pianist and his father owned a chain of theaters and cinemas. As a young boy, Barry helped his dad run his theaters, and while on the job, he took in hundreds of movies, developing an obsession for film. This union of movies and music perfectly suited Barry.

Play free with a little left-hand warm-up. Play the left hand alone at first to get familiar with the patterns. Those are called *arpeggios* (chords played one note at a time). Listen closely. When you hear that wind blowing, tide roaring, and your heart soaring, then it's time to add the right hand!

Walk before you run. Start at a slow speed (tempo) and work your way up. The right-hand *octaves* (notes played with the same note a scale above) need to be played with authority! After all, the style is marked "Majestically." After you've got those octaves down, speed up a little, but not too much. Have you ever seen the royal family running for the bus? Not a very majestic image, is it?

Don't be too free with your *triplets* (three notes spaced over two beats). Keep them even, otherwise they can sound like a quarter note and two eighth notes.

 Keep the pedal off the metal. Hold your hand down to sustain notes in the right hand. Using too much pedal will muddy the flow of left-hand bass notes.

Candle on the Water *(page 24)*

Whaddaya know? Another Disney film, another Academy Award nomination for Best Song! "Candle on the Water" is from Disney's rather obscure 1977 animated film *Pete's Dragon*. The song didn't win the prize — it lost to Debbie Boone's "You Light Up My Life." But the song's singer, Helen Reddy, re-arranged it and released it to pop radio, where it became a minor hit. The movie also received a nomination for Original Song Score but lost to *A Little Night Music*.

The song is written by composer Joel Hirschhorn and collaborator Al Kasha. Hirschhorn's songs have sold more than 90 million records, have been featured in 20 movies, and have been recorded by various artists, including Elvis. Hirschhorn's partnership with Kasha yielded a few major hits, most notably "The Morning After," written for the 1972 film *The Poseidon Adventure*. Legend has it that the two wrote "The Morning After" in less than 24 hours. The song was a #1 hit single in January of 1973 for singer Maureen McGovern.

Pete's Dragon has a rather sad history in comparison to its much happier and more successful animated film cousins at Disney. Not only did it not win anything, it lost many things, including its own minutes, in what could be called "the yo-yo diet" of *Pete's Dragon*. The film started out at 134 minutes in its original version, and then was edited to 121 minutes after the longer version failed to excite audiences. Editors chopped it again for home video rental, all the way down to 104 minutes, an excision that resulted in losing its Oscar-nominated song ("Candle on the Water") altogether. In 1980, Disney bumped it back up to 128 minutes again, only to see a television edit of the film lop off over 30 minutes!

 The first four bars are a classic example of an arpeggio. The right hand rolls the chords. Then see how the arpeggios shift to the left hand. Have some fun playing through them a bit to warm up. They should have a flowing feeling like, um, you guessed it, water!

Watch out! Although the key of C has no sharps or flats, accidentals do happen. A sharp or flat sign (♯ or ♭) next to a note is called an *accidental,* but the composer put it there intentionally, so keep your eyes on the musical road.

Keep it upbeat! The eighth note rest at the start of almost every phrase means the melody starts on the second beat (or *upbeat*) of a measure, as opposed to the first beat (the downbeat). It gives you a sense of motion. Also, it gives the singers a chance to take a deep breath. Take a breath there, too. Relax.

The Candy Man (page 30)

Sammy Davis Jr., the man who popularized this delightful tune by taking it to the top of the Hot 100 in June of 1972, didn't get a part in the original film version of *Willy Wonka and the Chocolate Factory*. Nor did he have anything to do with writing the tune, a task accomplished by Anthony Newley and Leslie Bricusse. But Davis loved the song so much that he incorporated it into his set and performed so effectively that it became one of his best-loved tunes and a signature song in his career. For the record, Aubrey Woods, who played Billy the Candy Shoppe owner in the film, sang the original version.

Newley and Bricusse had considerable success together, the former as a composer, pop singer, and actor, the latter as a lyricist. With Bricusse, Newley composed and starred in the hit Broadway musical, *Stop the World — I Want to Get Off*, for which he won a Tony® Award for Best Actor in a Musical. He and Bricusse combined for the many wonderful moments in *Willy Wonka and the Chocolate Factory*, including the jubilant "(I've Got A) Golden Ticket" performed by Jack Albertson and Peter Ostrum and the wistful "Pure Imagination," sung by Wonka himself, Gene Wilder. But it was Newley and Bricusse's "Candy Man" that emerged from the film to become lodged in our collective consciousness. And justifiably so, as Bricusse's lyrics and Newley's melody go together as well as, say, chocolate and peanut butter. "Who can take tomorrow / Dip it in a dream? Separate the sorrow and collect up all the cream?" Why, the candy man can, of course.

Musical notes, like chocolates in a Whitman's sampler, come in all different shapes and sizes. Be sure to keep the long notes long and the short notes short here. Variety is the key. Then mix in love and some spirit. It will make the world sound yummy.

Don't get messy. Keep it clean and bright. Use the pedal sparsely, mostly at the end of phrases.

 I got rhythm and so do you; dotted rhythm, that is. If you can hum this tune, you already know what dotted rhythms sound like. A dot after a note gives that note its own value plus half. When it's followed by a short note, it creates that jumpy, peppy feeling, just like candy does.

Edelweiss (page 27)

The song "Edelweiss" has become so closely linked to *The Sound of Music* that it's hard to imagine the film without it. But that's almost what happened. During tryouts for the musical, writer/composer Richard Rodgers felt that something was missing. He thought that perhaps the character of Captain von Trapp, played by actor Theodore Bikel on Broadway, needed a vehicle to more accurately express his feelings of loss as he bid farewell to his home country of Austria. His partner, Oscar Hammerstein, was battling stomach cancer at the time, but it didn't stop them from collaborating. Their dazzling creative partnership came through again, with one final song. In fact, they were so pleased with "Edelweiss," they decided to use it twice in Ernest Lehman's film adaptation — once when a more sensitive Captain von Trapp sings it with his kids in their family room, and again at the Salzburg Festival when the entire family exhorts the crowds to join in the song as a call for solidarity when the Nazis encircle the amphitheater. Both appearances of the song are powerful, for very different reasons. Indeed, the entire soundtrack of this presentation is virtually unassailable. A good guess would be that there aren't many adults left on the planet who haven't heard most of the tracks so generously offered up by Richard and Oscar: "Maria," "Sixteen Going On Seventeen," "Climb Ev'ry Mountain," "Do-Re-Mi," "My Favorite Things." Most musicals would settle for a single hit song, but the genius of Rodgers and Hammerstein managed nearly ten instantly recognizable classics. So don your wimple, strap on the lederhosen, and start thinking like an Austrian!

On a bittersweet note, "Edelweiss" ended up being the last song written by the team of Richard Rodgers and Oscar Hammerstein. Nine months after *The Sound of Music* debuted on Broadway, Hammerstein succumbed to his disease.

Be sure to let this one blossom nice and slowly! It's so important (not to speed up), in fact, that two different musical terms meaning slow down are used (*rit.* and *rall.*) both at the beginning and end!

Softly tiptoe through these, er, *edelweiss*. This wonderful arrangement starts quietly, swells a bit louder, and drifts dreamily back to very soft again.

Those squiggly lines you see (near the end of the piece) are called rolled chords or *arpeggios*. It means to just play the chords, from bottom to top (quickly), one note at time!

Endless Love (page 34)

Jade and David fall madly in love and do whatever they can to be together, which is a lot, but apparently not enough for these young teens. So the parents have to butt in and, as usual, they ruin everything, a house goes up in flames, authorities step in, and everyone ends up in tears, including us, because, well, it's sad after all and we love a good tearjerker. Italian director Franco Zeffirelli must have been a real romantic because there's a lot of long, languid gazing, and an uncharacteristic amount of restraint. The director, a polarizing figure on the arts and culture scene internationally, has been a member of the Italian Senate since 1996, representing the conservative party, a surprising political affiliation considering his titillating artistic output — from operas to biblical cinema ("Jesus of Nazareth," a TV mini-series from 1977) — and his openly gay orientation.

You can find a lot of interesting info on this film, despite the fact that it flopped at the box office. Brooke Shields, the 15-year-old Jade, falls in love with Martin Hewitt's David, who's 17. Hewitt apparently beat out Tom Cruise, who debuts in this film. (Play "Spot Tom Cruise!") Jami Gertz and James Spader also pop in. Anyway, while the film tanked, Lionel Richie's song became the biggest selling, most inescapable single of 1982, topping the charts for over two months that year.

In a duet with Diana Ross, Lionel Richie gives voice to this lovely slice of tenderness on the title track, a song that was nominated for an Academy Award for Best Original Song in 1982. You may have heard other renditions by names like Mariah and Luther, and Kenny Rogers, but none have the innocent soulfulness of Richie's original with Diana.

Get handy quickly! Your right hand shifts lower to play notes your left hand would normally play. It allows the left hand to go lower than usual. This neat technique continues throughout the song. Follow the markings closely so your left hand can hit those deep romantic tones.

Keep it in moderation, of course, volume-wise. Express yourself, like Lionel Richie does, in a smooth way, from moderately soft (*mp*) to moderately loud (*mf*). Don't miss that soft (*p*) marking at the very end!

For fun, quickly play the left-hand repeating patterns (those linked together in groups of four). If you know the fingering beforehand, playing it will be a snap!

The Exodus Song (page 40)

Ernest Gold, conducting the Sinfonia of London Orchestra, is responsible for the brilliant version of this song that you hear in the film *Exodus*. Gold wrote the score in 1960 and for his efforts won both an Oscar for Best Original Score and a Grammy for Song of the Year. A version of the song, an instrumental by the duo Ferrante & Teicher, peaked at #2 on the *Billboard* "Hot 100" in 1961. It has since been covered hundreds of times, from Pat Boone, who stuck lyrics on it and called it something else ("This Land of Mine") to Chet Atkins, who countrified it with his guitar.

Otto Preminger's film *Exodus* concerned the historical events leading to the creation of the state of Israel. The film's all-star cast included Paul Newman, Eva Marie Saint, Ralph Richardson, Peter Lawford, and Lee J. Cobb. Gold was clearly moved by the subject matter of *Exodus*, as he was inspired to write a score that was as intense as it was sincere. He had plenty of time to do it as well. Rather than jumping in to score the movie after it was shot, Gold was hired during pre-production and was present during the entire process, which meant he spent a year on the film, an incredible luxury for a movie composer.

When Gold embarked on the project, he'd just come off a triumph with his 1959 film *On the Beach*, for which he earned a Golden Globe for Best Original Score. In all, Gold earned four Oscar nominations and three Golden Globe nominations during his musical career, which lasted 45 years.

Gold can also take credit for a successful offspring. His son Andrew Gold enjoyed a pretty fruitful career himself, writing and performing songs like the Top 10 single "Lonely Boy" in 1977 and "Thank You for Being a Friend" (any *Golden Girls* fans out there?) in 1978.

This music rolls along grandly thanks partly to *rolled chords*, which are played quickly, one note at a time. You see a twisted or squiggly line next to them. The first occurs in the 7th measure (under the lyric "ancient") and there are several more throughout. Play them a couple times and you'll be on a "roll" when they appear!

Thunder rumbles with rapidly alternating notes *(tremolos)* when there are three bars between notes. The first tremolo comes after the lyric "children can run free." The second one is at the very end of the song. Both get louder but the second is extra loud and accented *(ffz)* so dig in and stake your claim.

After a very loud introduction *(ff)*, the dynamics change to moderately soft *(mp)* for one verse. The next two verses are moderately loud *(mf)* and the ending very loud and accented *(ffz)* so have fun conducting this piece, maestro!

Forrest Gump - Main Title (Feather Theme) (page 48)

Pop music plays a huge role in the lovable *Forrest Gump* film. Like *American Graffiti*, this film courses through three decades of American pop music, beginning with Elvis Presley's "Hound Dog," and touching on classics like Aretha Franklin's "Respect," The Mamas and The Papas' "California Dreamin'," and Simon and Garfunkel's "Mrs. Robinson." Yet, while those songs take up much of Forrest's screen time, there is another musical matter that is, in my humble opinion, just as significant — Alan Silvestri's genius score.

Silvestri, who grew up in Teaneck, New Jersey, wasn't born into a musical family. In fact, he had to wait until he was in his 20s before he heard a symphony orchestra. Despite the odds, he picked up drumming as a young boy and taught himself guitar and various brass and woodwind instruments. He dreamt of being a jazz musician, which led him to Berklee, where he began composing his own music. The rest, as they say, is history. Silvestri has since scored such films as the *Back to the Future* trilogy, *Romancing the Stone*, *Who Framed Roger Rabbit*, and a dozen other successful films. Silvestri earned an Oscar nomination, and won a Grammy for his song "Believe," from his score for *The Polar Express*. He won another Grammy for the music from *Cast Away*.

His talent, critics and fans say, lies in his ability to intuit the deepest understanding of a film, and somehow produce music that matches that understanding. In *Forrest Gump*, a lovable Tom Hanks stumbles and bumbles his way through the most significant milestones of the modern era. The film itself, based on a 1986 novel of the same name by Winston Groom, earned 13 Academy Award nominations, including one for Silvestri for Best Original Score. The film went on to win six awards, capturing the hearts of the world in the process.

The surprise in this box of chocolates is two treble clefs. You read the lower notes as if they were on the top staff. So the first note you play is A, which happens to be the key!

Those fascinating rhythms go together, so for faster learning, hop down to the second line where the right hand comes in, and play those two rhythms at the same time!

Soft and sweet is the tone of this piece, just like the movie. There is one loud section, however. It's easy to find. Hint: Look where the sharp (♯) signs disappear! The key changes there too, naturally!

The *8va* marking you see means to play the notes one octave higher. A scale has eight notes, the eighth note the same pitch as the first, just higher-sounding. If in doubt whether you have the right note, listen closely and play it by ear.

Georgia on My Mind (page 52)

By 1930 Hoagy Carmichael had already written more than a dozen songs, but without success. His most famous work, "Star Dust" was published and recorded in 1929 but didn't find an audience. While toiling at an investment company in New York for income, Carmichael composed songs in his spare time. One solemn, idea-less afternoon, Carmichael's friend and saxophonist Frankie Trumbauer made a suggestion: "Why don't you write a song about Georgia? Nobody ever lost money writing songs about the South." The eloquent, longing ballad has since become a national treasure and embedded in America's collective musical memory.

Chart research indicates that Trumbauer hit the Top Ten with "Georgia" way back in 1931. But it was, of course, Ray Charles, the "Genius of Soul," who popularized it. In fact, folks have come to link Charles in their imaginations with his heartwarming rendition, which hit #1 in September of 1960. Over the next 40 years, this "old sweet song" did remain Ray's signature piece (he was born in Georgia, so it made some sense), on its way to becoming Georgia's official state song in 1979. Charles' version, done quickly in just four studio takes, won Grammy Awards for Best Male Vocal Recording and Best Pop Song Performance. The album also won for Best Male Vocal Performance Album, and another song on the same album, "Let the Good Times Roll," won for Best R&B Performance. At the same time, Charles' version appeared in 1966 in the film *The Big T.N.T. Show*, a concert film.

A rather compelling debate ensues when enthusiasts of the song discuss whether it's about the state of Georgia, or "Georgia," as in a woman. Carmichael and Gorrell kept it purposely ambiguous, contributing to its mystery and magnificent allure.

Learn this entire song! A beautiful introduction precedes the famous chorus we all know so well. Impress your friends by playing the whole song through!

Scan those cool guitar chords (above the melody) to see where it's all happening, dude! Those measures, where you see two or three chord changes, are worth a fun test-drive. When you start playing they'll already be on your mind.

Please don't attempt a fast version of this song! The only marking is slowly. Express yourself, for sure, but, if you speed this up, a Georgian may send a flying peach your way!

Ghost (page 43)

If *Ghost* is not a typical romantic comedy, with its otherworldly love story between poor dead Sam and lonely potter Molly, then Maurice Jarre's score of the film is equally atypical. Most fans fondly recall the powerful usage of Alex North's gorgeous "Unchained Melody," sung famously by The Righteous Brothers. But Jarre's romantic motif, which signals the couple's loving relationship, contains almost as much potency. The use of the Righteous Brothers song in the film — the reason why legions flocked to record stores to buy the album — is nearly overshadowed by North's passionate instrumental version of the song and Jarre's moving love theme, both of which bring tremendous emotional weight to the scenes involving Sam (his ghost, actually), and Molly.

Nominated for an Academy Award, Jarre's score is typical of his best work, which includes *Lawrence of Arabia* and *Doctor Zhivago*. But unlike the broad, sweeping work of those celluloid epics, his soundtrack for *Ghost* is more intimate and slightly more experimental. It was, after all, the '80s when he composed this material — synthesizers were beginning to dominate pop music — and Jarre showed an affinity for changing with the times. Many say that during the end credits, in which this theme in all its harmonic grandeur is allowed to ring out unrestrained, suggests Jarre's *Lawrence of Arabia* days. After spinning this for a while, I agree.

Expression is the mainstay of this longing lament. Smooth motion means blending, not blurring, one note into the next with no pause, only a linger. This linking is also called *legato*. Listen closely to hear one note fade as the next arises. To know if it's right . . . trust the old saying: play it by ear.

Chill out a bit when it comes to *tempo* (speed). No marching band number here, nor tubas rocking back and forth! Be like an orchestra conductor, sensing the flow of the notes, finding moments. Slow down and speed up but don't abandon the beat, just tweak. Humans breathe, sway, and dance, and unlike metronomes we know when something touches the heart or feels right, as does this beautiful tone poem.

Don't get hooked on a feeling. Let the emotions move and change, reflecting an orchestral, epic feel with accents on shifts between long and short notes. Also, highlight the *triplets* (three notes played on one or two beats) adding a wisp of hesitation. Then let grandeur shine on big chords.

Find your voice! *Voicing*, on a simple level, makes some notes louder than others. This makes a *phrase*. Try the *melody line* (usually the top notes) alone, first with your right hand. Once you've got that, add the underlying notes (the accompaniment), making sure they're softer. Melody is almost always loudest. However, *do* give extra voicing to the cool bass line or neat chords. This makes a great singer, or pianist, as that is *your* voice.

A Hard Day's Night (page 56)

As strange as it may seem, the one *Hard Day's Night* song that the Beatles didn't actually perform in the movie was the title track! The tune wasn't recorded until a week before shooting of the film wrapped up. The opening scene in which the song was intended to play, where the mop tops tumble and frolic, had already been shot and so the situation sealed its fate as a soundtrack-only cut.

The score for the film, which also included Beatles' classics like "If I Fell," "All My Loving," and "She Loves You," was nominated for both an Oscar (Best Score) and a Grammy (Best Original Score for a Motion Picture). When the film itself came out at the height of Beatlemania, critics tripped over themselves attempting to lavish praise on it. A remarkable fact, considering it took only four months from the first day of filming to its premiere. Others say that the film, directed by Richard Lester and named by *Time* magazine as one of the Top 100 films of all time, with its cinematic devices like handheld cameras and quick cutting, spawned the field of music videos! When the movie was made, The Beatles' fame hadn't yet spread, so the executives at United Artists were determined to keep costs down, which is why it's filmed hastily in black and white rather than in color.

You won't sleep, either, with this great beat! The left hand boogies, literally. Put the accent on the quarter notes in a boogie-woogie bass. It's accented 2/2 time, so count the measures one, two, one, two.

Don't miss those great blue notes. Blues players love minor intervals (where the top note is lowered). Therefore, F♯, when flatted, is F natural. Accent that flatted B (B♭), at the lyric "feel all right" . . . and you will too!

A bridge section, at the lyric, "When I'm home," loses the blues feeling for a moment. Soften the beat and tone here, like The Beatles did. Don't worry, you'll soon get back, Jo-jo, to the blues.

I Am a Man of Constant Sorrow (page 61)

"I Am a Man of Constant Sorrow" has been recorded by many well-known recording artists, as well as the Soggy Bottom Boys in the 2000 film *O Brother, Where Art Thou?* Pretty famous song, then, right? So it comes as a bit of a surprise that its author, Dick Burnett, can't actually remember writing it. Part of the problem was that the song is really old. If Burnett did write it, he called it something else ("The Farewell Song") and he penned it way back in 1913. What we do know is that Burnett was born way back in 1883 and he was blinded in 1907, which might explain the "sorrow" part. Some feel he may have adapted an older song with new lyrics.

The Stanley Brothers, a well-known bluegrass group, popularized the song back in 1950. But the song gained an entirely new life when the singer-songwriters of the '60s picked up on it. Bob Dylan interpreted it on his self-titled debut in 1962. Waylon Jennings recorded it on his solo debut in 1966, and Rod Stewart included it on *his* solo debut in 1969. The fact that these very forward-thinking artists covered such a traditional, backcountry tune disproved the idea that non-pop music alienated audiences. This was underscored when the wonderful soundtrack to *O Brother* sold over eight million copies and snared the Grammy Award for Album of the Year.

The Soggy Bottom Boys, featuring Dan Tyminski, Harley Allen, and Pat Enright, had a nice run with the Burnett song thanks to its cameo in the film, winning a CMA Award for Single of the Year and a Grammy Award for Best Country Collaboration with Vocals. Not bad for a fictitious outfit!

Marked "moderately fast country," this toe-tapper is nice and peppy, to keep even occasional sorrow away.

Move it on over, so the right hand (R.H.) can shift down and play some sweet lower notes. Follow those right hand shift markings throughout and this bluegrass classic will sprout!

To get into character, slap your knee or stomp your foot a couple times before you start. This accented 2/2 time (two beats per measure) indicates sorrow interrupted by dancing.

 Bluegrass, a form of country, uses both flatted notes and open chords to make that lonesome sound. Open chords leave out the middle note. Lowered (flatted) notes are blues-based but bluegrass is named after Kentucky, the Bluegrass State!

I Will Always Love You (page 64)

What a journey *this* tune has had! Dolly Parton originally wrote the song back in 1973 and it was released a year later on her hit album *Jolene*. Since then, Parton has told interviewers she was inspired to write the song for her former business partner and mentor Porter Wagoner, with whom she had a falling out. The song was released as a follow-up single, after the chart-topping success of the title track, in April 1974. The single reached #1 on the country chart in May, but had just modest success on the pop charts. Parton re-recorded the song in 1982 for the soundtrack to the film *The Best Little Whorehouse in Texas*. That version also reached #1 on the Country chart, marking the first time the same song by the same artist reached #1 twice. Dolly recorded the song a third time, as a duet with country star Vince Gill, and the song peaked at #15 in December of 1995.

On the pop side, the song was most famously featured in the 1992 film *The Bodyguard*, sung by Whitney Houston in her film debut. Houston was originally slated to record Jimmy Ruffin's "What Becomes of the Brokenhearted," as the film's lead single. But when producer Lawrence Kasdan discovered the song was already included in *Fried Green Tomatoes*, co-star Kevin Costner set out to find a new song. He brought executives this song, only in the form of Linda Ronstadt's 1975 cover version of the tune from her album *Prisoner in Disguise*. (He thought that revealing the song's country music origin would color their impressions of it.) In a hotel ballroom one night, Houston recorded a few takes of the song, reinterpreting it as a soul ballad to showcase her voice. Two decades after Parton's original emerged, Houston's version of the single sold over 15 million copies. It became a regular on countdown lists, appearing at #8 on VH1's "100 Greatest Songs of the Past 25 Years," #4 on VH1's "100 Greatest Songs of the 90s" and #1 on VH1's "100 Greatest Love Songs." In 2003, CMT ranked it #16 on their "100 Greatest Songs in Country Music." In 2004, CMT ranked it #1 on their "100 Greatest Country Love Songs." Parton's work stands as one of the most covered songs ever written. And that's not even counting all the weddings!

Keep up your speed *(tempo)* a bit in this heartfelt love song. Although marked slowly, keep it moving steadily. Play the opening section *freely*. Then maintain a regular tempo, holding back a little. A beautiful bittersweet sentiment is held within this goodbye/love song. The poignant moment and graceful exit portray the simple wonder of Dolly Parton's overlooked musical genius and create a country music *Casablanca* moment, the tale of one who denies himself love for the sake of another and a greater good.

The volume *(dynamics)* of this star-crossed love tune swells and recedes as marked. To avoid having a steadily louder wall of sound, note the markings: *mp*, *mf*, *f*, and *ff*. These respectively mean moderately soft, moderately loud, loud, and very loud. Return to the quiet moments when needed. The power of emotion is both soft and loud, so let your heart whisper and wail!

The last chorus raises the bar to the next level. A classic technique to pump any ending is called *taking it up a key*. Notice how the key of A major becomes B major (three sharps become five sharps). Play a run-through of the final chorus so you'll be ready to bring the fireworks.

Although all songs in this book play fine as is on any regular (analog) piano, digital pianos also have a transpose button (which magically *changes keys* for you). Here's how it works. You play the written notes . . . and the digital piano makes them sound in a different key. So, next time a singer says take it up a key, maestro, hit the transpose button and say name your key. Those allergic to technology pay this no mind! Isn't it best to play the songs and have fun?

Il Postino (The Postman) *(page 72)*

Argentine composer Luis Enriquez Bacalov wrote the acclaimed score for the 1994 romance, *Il Postino*, which won an Academy Award for Best Original Score. Not to be confused with the Kevin Costner, post-apocalyptic film of the same name (*The Postman*), *Il Postino* is a pastoral and low-key, but passionate, movie about the relationship between a worldly Chilean poet, Pablo Neruda, and his rather sheltered friend, Mario, a postman in a sleepy Italian fishing village. The two acquaintances strike up a friendship, and Neruda, in exile from his country, helps his friend understand the beauty of poetry, knowledge he uses to successfully communicate his feelings for a pretty village girl.

Bacalov's score for this poignant picture works perfectly with the serene quietude of the locale. His considerable experience and lengthy resume enabled him to adapt his work to virtually any scenario. In fact, he may be the only composer whose work ranged from the Biblical (the Academy Award-nominated *The Gospel According to Saint Matthew* in 1967), to spaghetti westerns *(Storm Rider, Django)*, to having his work ("Motorcycle Circus") placed in the Quentin Tarantino slasher pic *Kill Bill* (2003/04). But it doesn't stop there. Many who know Bacalov's work best suggest that he did his top stuff for his collaborations with Italian progressive rock bands New Trolls, Osanna, and Il Rovescio della Medaglia. In 1971 the New Trolls released the album *Concerto Grosso No. 1*, with classical music arrangements written by Bacalov. This avant-garde adventure has come to be considered one of the most important Italian rock 'n' roll recordings ever made.

Like a relaxing tea, this mellow, moving favorite needs to be savored slowly. With lots of long measures and held notes, the moderate *(moderato)* tempo instruction is there mostly to keep you going! Although not slow-motion, this one is a gently flowing river.

No need to shout at this postman! He's a good listener and he delivers letters softly (*p*), a little louder (*mp*) and super soft (*ppp*) at the end. Read between the lines (staves) too, and find arrows marking slight dynamic changes.

Hit those high notes running! Some notes soar above the five-line staff. Those little lines up above the staff (called *ledger lines*) help count how high the note is! Be patient, soon you won't need to count. You'll just read it like a postcard!

No need to take Italian lessons. *Lento* means slow, *mosso* is moving, and *a tempo* just means to go back to the same speed as before! Now, that's *bene* (good)!

The John Dunbar Theme (page 76)

When composer extraordinaire John Barry emerged from a two-year absence due to illness, he came back healthy and produced the soundtrack to *Dances with Wolves*, a dazzling work that includes the Oscar-winning "John Dunbar Theme." Not only that, Barry, reinvigorated and inspired, nearly single-handedly redefined the then flagging genre of the Western. Suddenly, with the success of *Wolves*, Hollywood once again believed in the commercial viability of "Cowboys and Indians."

Compositionally, Barry's work soars, capturing the soul-searching spirit of the film. He gives each character a theme, while at the same time shifting tone, color, and tempo to paint the inner portrait of John Dunbar, the film's main character played by Kevin Costner. Dunbar's soul-searching journey across the American frontier allows Barry to explore mood, evocative situations, and the profoundly emotional conflicts raging across the screen. Barry's Dunbar theme is, arguably, the most beautiful work he's ever done, with its characteristically epic sweep and gorgeous string arrangement.

Barry fans often make the argument that his work salvages this film, which, at three hours in length, can — I'll admit it — be a little tedious. But when those strings and that brass enter the picture the entire experience gains added dimension and truly comes to life. This is the aim of every great score and Barry did it better throughout his career than nearly everyone. The Academy thought so, too, bestowing him in 1991 with the Academy Award for Best Original Score.

Don't howl or race through this majestic heartstring puller. Gentle and graceful is the tone. Steady and moderate is the pace. Be sure to start with a nice slow speed *(tempo)*. You might surprise yourself and find your preferred groove right at that meter. In that case, why rush through life?

Don't be fooled into playing a fascinating rhythm with the left hand. The *dotted pattern* (the dot after a note) sometimes indicates a jumpin' dance feel, *but not here*. Even though a short note follows, make the pattern steady like the tolling of a large bell. Remember, the slower speed allows more sustained notes. If you see folks bopping around the dance floor, that's a sure sign to tone it down!

The *D.S. al Coda* marking means go back, Jack! Go back in the music and find the funny-looking 𝄋 sign (that's the *S* in *D.S.*) and play from there to the *Coda*. The *Coda* is the funny-looking 𝄌 sign. So, it basically means: Go back, then play from the 𝄋 to the *Coda*. Italian musical terms are not difficult at all, and certainly no secret "code-a." They are fun, helpful, and easy the second time around!

Opt. 8va means play the same notes one octave higher. Everything stays the same except it moves up. For example, the F note is still F, it's just the next F above. So play the exact same thing higher, and brave those altitudes. After all, if you don't like the view, it's optional.

Theme from "Jurassic Park" (page 80)

The creative partnership of director Steven Spielberg and composer John Williams has produced more smash hits than a major league baseball team. Okay, maybe a *bad* baseball team, but still . . . Williams and Spielberg have combined on an astonishing list of tremendous cinematic successes. Here's how the story goes: Williams had already established himself in Hollywood — winning an Oscar for his work on *Fiddler on the Roof* — when an upstart Spielberg approached Williams to score his 1974 film, *Jaws*. That film earned Williams his second Oscar. Enter Spielberg partner George Lucas, who then hired Williams for his *Star Wars* saga, leading to his third Oscar. Needless to say, this Oscar dominance placed John Williams atop the short list of the day's composers. With Spielberg's simultaneous rise, the two superstars ascended to the pinnacle of Hollywood achievement, including *Close Encounters of the Third Kind*, *Superman*, *E.T.*, and the *Indiana Jones* films. The team continued to pair on more recent films, like *Schindler's List*, *Saving Private Ryan*, *War of the Worlds*, *Munich*, and many other critically important films.

Williams' work is rooted in the classical tradition, inspired mainly by the style of the Late Romantics like Mahler and Strauss. Occasionally, he filters in more modern overtones. But he never loses his audience. He understands the importance of accessibility, and his best work is filled with melodic hooks, exciting fanfare, and enjoyable marches. Like all the great film scorers, Williams is highly esteemed for his dexterity in conjuring a sound that perfectly complements the mood of a film.

Jurassic Park, the most successful film of all time, also represents the first suspense movie since *Jaws* that featured the work of the Williams and Spielberg team. "Theme from *Jurassic Park*," though, doesn't have anything close to the menace and peril insinuated by that iconic killer shark motif. Instead, it's characterized by a more lush and hopeful wistfulness. Learn it and see!

Hail, *caesura!* Those early double slash marks (//) indicate an audible pause.

Does anybody really know what time (signature) it is? Notice that 6/4 (six quarter notes per measure) becomes 3/4 and 4/4. John Williams does this to change the feel of the beat a little. There are more time signature changes, so watch like a hawk — or a pterodactyl.

Be the leader of the band, when it comes to speed and volume changes. Like a conductor, watch for tempo and dynamics markings. Your nodding head and nimble fingers are conductor and orchestra, but no need to hold a baton in your teeth.

Legends of the Fall (page 69)

Often, setting plays a huge role in establishing the musical themes of a motion picture. In the case of producer Edward Zwick's film *Legends of the Fall*, the big sky country of Montana assumes a central role and composer James Horner takes advantage of its breathtaking presence.

Horner derives inspiration from the majestic plains and mountains of the landscape and his technique produces some of the best work of his career, a significant achievement considering *Braveheart*, *Glory*, and *Titanic*.

Horner employs dramatic themes for the film's characters, also called *leitmotifs*. Horner adapts and alters these leitmotifs — from simple and elemental to elegant and orchestral — depending on the intensity of the scene in which it appears. It's the strength of the themes that contributes to *Legends'* overall success. Yet while those recurring themes bolster the soundtrack, Horner's main theme remains with the viewer long after the closing credits. Introduced in the latter half of the film, the theme focuses not on a character but on the broader representation of the story and landscape and serves as the emotional heart of the score. Throughout the soundtrack, Horner makes use of the fabulous London Symphony Orchestra, as well as fiddle and Japanese wood flute that will remind listeners of *Glory* and *Titanic*. Horner's detailed work might also take your mind off the rather strange performance turned in by Brad Pitt.

It's as easy as *one*, *two*, *three*, *four* in this moderately-paced and beautiful ballad. A steady saddle keeps the 4/4 rolling along. However, watch for *two* measures of 2/4 near the end! Like a deep musical breath, *two strong beats* replace the 4/4. Take a moment there, on the smooth trail, to breathe clean country air. Let the melody linger before the eagle soars into the horizon!

A sharp eye notices a slight key change early on (in the tenth bar or *measure*). G sharp falls, turning the key from A to D. Don't worry, both keys are similar. Everything else, including the mood, speed, and volume stay exactly the same, too, so forge ahead with one less sharp but plenty of pioneer spirit!

Put your left hand through the paces, in preparation to head off tricky spots at the pass! Make *Lefty*, your left hand, a ready and strong gunslinger instead of an old cowboy!

Express wide open grand spaces by following *dynamics* and *tempo* changes. The soft opening (*p*) grows to medium loud (*mf*), softens (*decresc.*) and slows (*rit.*) very gradually. But hold those horses, because as speed returns (*a tempo*) so does the volume (*mf*), until they both ride off into the sunset slow and soft (*rit. e dim.*).

A Man and a Woman
(Un homme et une femme) (page 84)

When a film relies less on dialogue and more on its visual cinematography to communicate, it puts much more emphasis on its score. This happens with the French classic *A Man and a Woman*, a breathtaking exposition of visual imagery. Directed by Claude Lelouche and released in 1966, the film demonstrates how beautifully screen images can work together with a gorgeously rendered score. In fact, the union worked so well it dominated awards ceremonies from 1966 through 1968, winning the Palme d'Or at Cannes, Oscars for Best Original Screenplay and Best Foreign Language Film, and a Golden Globe for Best Foreign Language film, among other honors. It put French director Claude Lelouch on the map and earned wads of money on a very small budget. Not only that, it proved to be very influential to subsequent moviemakers. One can clearly see *A Man and a Woman* as the mother of everything from 1970's *Love Story* to more modern fare like *When Harry Met Sally*.

Composed by Francis Lai, the music featured in *A Man and a Woman* (the first of many collaborations between Lai and Lelouche) underscores the director's poignant storyline, which follows the courtship of Anne and Jean-Louis, who meet at their kids' boarding school. It's unclear what's happened to them in the past, but they've both clearly suffered gaping emotional wounds, and they find solace and a desperate sort of love in each other. Lai's loose and low-key music makes a brilliant companion to Lelouche's handheld filming and raw aesthetic.

You can leave your hat on, just like the first three notes. That symbol is called *a fermata* and it means you decide how long to hold those notes.

Read the lyrics once aloud. Like men and women, words and music come together, but it takes a little while. Notice how the accented words come together, not at first, but at the ends of lines, "night" and "tight." To leave no doubt this is a budding courtship, the longer notes seal the deal.

Love is about good timing, so don't miss the 2/4 time signature change that accents "lonely night" and "very tight". Love is fickle, however, and it goes right back to 4/4.

The Man From Snowy River (Main Title Theme) (page 119)

Some scores evoke romance, some might give goose bumps with a haunting vibe, others still might stir up feelings of peace and beauty. Bruce Rowland's soundtrack to the Australian film *The Man from Snowy River* is an exhilarating call to arms, a soaring, heraldic theme that not only recalls the grand landscapes of its setting, but also serves as a triumphant coming of age. To give you some idea of its success as a creative endeavor, the score has been generously multi-purposed since its 1982 debut in the film. Rowland also composed a special version of the main theme of *The Man from Snowy River Suite*, to be used for the Opening Ceremony of the 2000 Summer Olympics, which happened to be held in Sydney, Australia that year. For good reason, Rowland's tune has made its greatest inroads in Australia. He composed exclusive arrangements of this and other tunes for a 2002 musical theater production called *The Man from Snowy River: Arena Spectacular* and an original cast album of that production that won an Australian Grammy, also known as an ARIA. *The Man from Snowy River* spawned a sequel, 1988's *Return to Snowy River*.

The idea for the movie came from a poem by Australian Andrew Barton "Banjo" Paterson in 1890. Paterson, you most likely *don't* know, was the man behind the classic "Waltzing Matilda," which became one of Australia's most famous tunes. Typically, Paterson's work represented a sweet, romantic view of rural Australia. His "The Man from Snowy River" captured the imagination of his nation as well. As a result of this national affection, Paterson's image appears on the Australian $10 bill, along with an illustration inspired by his "Snowy River" poem and, as part of the copy-protection microprint, the text of the actual poem.

Find the source of this flowing music by accenting the melody. The beautiful tune, contained in the top notes, should be a little louder than the rest. This technique is called *voicing*.

No meandering on this river, get the order straight. Review the structure, which contains returns *(codas)*, to keep this one going smoothly downstream.

Sound the trumpets for this grand tune. This moderately loud (*mf*) piece has an orchestral feel. So, let this river run boldly!

This river ride rolls and glides. A squiggly line between two notes (a *glissando*) means glide and the same line next to a chord means it's rolled (an *arpeggio*).

Mission: Impossible Theme (page 121)

A few bars is all it takes. In fact, you could probably "name that tune" in just two or three notes, to co-opt a popular game show phrase. That's how identifiable and unique Lalo Schifrin's "Mission: Impossible" theme is. His taut, flute-laced, jazz-based music virtually defines the fanciful action and espionage, in what could only be called a perfect marriage of movie (and TV show) and music. Schifrin's theme has, over time, become more popular than the screen versions of the show it introduced, an incredible accomplishment and a testament to the power of a truly memorable motif. Originally known as "The Fuse," the theme had been intended for a "chase" portion of the show. But creator Bruce Geller liked it so much better than Schifrin's original opening theme that he used it there instead.

To the average moviegoer, the name Lalo Schifrin most likely means very little. But his scores have graced some of the generation's most famous movies, including *Cool Hand Luke*, *Dirty Harry*, and *Bullitt*. The son of the concertmaster of the Buenos Aires Philharmonic, Schifrin served as pianist and arranger for Dizzy Gillespie in the late '50s and he moved permanently to New York City in the early '60s. There he began scoring films. Oscar nominations followed, six in all (not to mention 21 Grammy nominations!), including two in the '70s: *Voyage of the Damned* and *The Amityville Horror*. And speaking of Schifrin's work in the '70s, he had been contracted to score William Friedkin's frightfest *The Exorcist*. But after he produced and submitted six minutes for the film's trailer, it was rejected after scaring the living daylights out of audiences. Schifrin's final score was also rejected, though good money says it's a corker!

In 1996, when a remake of the film *Mission: Impossible*, starring Tom Cruise, was released, Adam Clayton and Larry Mullen of U2 introduced a whole new generation of listeners to Schifrin's exhilarating blast. Their cover of the song hit the Top 10 on the *Billboard* "Hot 100."

Your mission, should you decide to accept it . . . is to play five beats per measure and have fun doing it! The time signature is 5/4 combined with left hand accents (upside down carets) in the bass line. Have no fear. It's possible!

Don't let this slick suspenseful tune self-destruct. Play the left hand portion a few times before you start, to get the pattern and accents down. Look out! The second accent comes on the off-beat, so don't let it escape.

Spy those graceful triplets as the famous melody appears. A number three, below the notes, means they are played in one beat.

 Don't tiptoe. Drive this tricked-out sports car fairly fast and loud enough to be heard on a hidden microphone. The volume goes from moderately loud (*mf*) to very loud (*ff*), as if creating a diversion to steal some diamonds!

Moon River *(page 123)*

Holly Golightly sits comfortably on the fire escape of her New York City tenement house, a half-size guitar in her lap, her hair tied coquettishly in a wide ivory bow. Dreamily, she strums the chords to "Moon River," attracting the attention of Paul Varjak, a writer who throws open his window to see where that lovely voice is coming from. When Varjak, played by George Peppard, hears Holly, played by Audrey Hepburn, the seeds of romance are sown. It is unsurprising that they connect via "Moon River," one of the greatest love songs ever written.

Johnny Mercer and Henry Mancini wrote the song. Mercer, a successful songwriter who'd experienced a drought through the rock and roll years, desperately sought a hit to boost his career. He'd won a couple of Academy Awards for Best Song for "On the Atchison, Topeka, and the Santa Fe," which appeared in the 1946 flick *The Harvey Girls*, and another for "In the Cool, Cool, Cool of the Evening" in *Here Comes the Groom* (1951). Mancini is, of course, one of the most successful composers in the history of popular music. He was nominated for an unprecedented 72 Grammys, winning 20, and he earned 18 Academy Award nominations, winning four, including two with Mercer for "Moon River" in 1961. The next year, the two combined for another Academy Award, this time for the main theme in *Days of Wine and Roses*.

An instrumental version of "Moon River" is played over the film's opening title. Mercer's lyrics are heard in the fire escape performance. Incredibly, talk of removing the Hepburn song scene from the film arose in the offices of the Paramount movie studio. But when the young Hepburn heard the rumors she stormed the office, either saying "over my dead body," or threatening some unenviable fate on someone, depending on whose account you read. Actually, Hepburn's version was not included on the original soundtrack album. Mancini and his chorus cut a considerably more lavish, easy listening version as a single and it became a Top 40 hit. After Hepburn's death in 1993, Warner Brothers released a version of it on the *Music from the Films of Audrey Hepburn* project.

Pedal down this river, using your trusty sustain pedal, letting those notes linger like your Huckleberry friend on a raft!

Don't hit any whitewater rapids on this slow boat to mellow. Float gently, tempo-wise, and even slow it down a little more at the end *(rall.)*.

Steady as she goes on the volume. A moderately loud dynamic (*mf*) keeps this craft focused on that sweet melody.

Sneak a peek ahead for *arpeggios*. Arpeggios are rolled chords, from the bottom up, marked by a squiggly line. No tidal wave though, just a smooth flourish!

The Music of Goodbye (page 131)

The original score for the hit film *Out of Africa*, written by John Barry, contained a lovely instrumental that lyricists Marilyn and Alan Bergman appended with some lyrics. Executives rush-released "The Music of Goodbye" as a single and music video *after* the movie had been out for a while. Barry, the composer behind *Born Free* and over a dozen James Bond scores, won an Academy Award for Best Original Score, and the soundtrack received a high ranking (#15) on the American Film Institute's "100 Years of Film Scores."

Barry's score for the 1986 film is the epitome of his post-Bond romantic style. With its long, shimmering notes on high strings and embellishments by muted brass and woodwind melodies, the soundtrack echoes the lush themes he penned for films like *Somewhere in Time*, *High Road to China*, and *Dances with Wolves.* The score to *Out of Africa* is actually something of a hodge-podge. It also features some Mozart, some traditional African songs, and a few second-generation compositions from Barry, songs repurposed from his older material (including snippets from *Born Free*) and rearranged by director Sydney Pollack. Together, the whole works even greater than the sum of its parts, as it sweeps listeners and viewers away to the veldt of Africa, and into the hearts of its passionate main characters, Karen Blixen and Denys Finch Hatton.

This sentimental ballad uses a double bar line to mark the end of the introduction. Linger there for a moment before wishing it goodbye.

Sing with your fingers. The melody is very expressive, so use phrasing, and little changes in volume and speed to let the emotion flow.

Don't shout out this soft and tender goodbye! Keep the volume moderately soft (*mp*). The *tempo* (speed) stays medium-slow and steady too.

For you aspiring songwriters, see how the melody uses intervals to express longing by constantly jumping either seven or nine notes. Because *octaves* (eight note intervals) symbolize order and stability, missing them (with sevenths and ninths) creates a feeling of goodbye.

My Heart Will Go On (Love Theme from 'Titanic') (page 135)

Composer James Horner originally wrote this tune as an instrumental, a musical motif slated to appear in several scenes of the 1997 James Cameron blockbuster, *Titanic*. But when Horner realized the beauty and effectiveness of the tune, he proposed to Cameron that they run a full vocal version of the song during the movie. At first Cameron rejected the idea, fearing that it would be perceived as too commercial, but that didn't deter Horner from recruiting lyricist Will Jennings to pen some words.

Horner's next obstacle was convincing popular singer Celine Dion to sing those words. Initially, Dion declined the invitation, but her manager/husband, Rene Angelil, coaxed his wife into demoing the track. Once Horner received the demo, he waited for just the right moment to present it to Cameron. After hearing it a handful of times, the director approved its usage for the film's end credits.

This back and forth between Cameron and Horner wasn't unusual. Their last project together, the 1986 film *Aliens*, resulted in near disaster. Due largely to tight filming schedules and deadlines, Horner had barely enough time to complete the soundtrack and was said to have not seen the film before composing its music. After that experience, Horner assumed that he and the Canadian-American director would never collaborate again. (Surprisingly, *Aliens* earned Horner his first Academy Award nomination for Best Original Score.) But after hearing Horner's subsequent work for 1995's *Braveheart*, Cameron had a change of heart and invited Horner in once again to work on *Titanic*.

This melody touches all hearts so let it ring out! The wonderful, rich arrangement boasts a flutter of notes. Remember to make them sit snugly, in their places, beneath, around, and supporting the melody. All the rest will go on fine!

Two unlikely keys unite in the musical affair. Note the four sharps (F♯, C♯, G♯, and D♯) as the piece begins in the key of E. Later notice the four flats (B♭, E♭, A♭, and D♭) that take us to closure, in the key of A♭. Play the flatted and raised notes once or twice to make the transition smoothly through the passionate leap.

Skip the introduction for now. Try jumping to where the vocal melody comes in. Then go back later to the opening measures with a soaring heart and spirit, ready to navigate the lively, ornate prelude to this timeless song of everlasting affection.

Go quietly. There is a long quieting period at the end. Watch for the marking (*ff decrescendo to end*) and peak the volume there. Then begin softening until you reach the final chimes. But do remember that volume builds throughout, so start softly and intensify this affair!

On Golden Pond (page 126)

Throughout his career, Dave Grusin has written and arranged scores for nearly 100 movies and television shows, including *The Graduate*, *The Goodbye Girl*, *Reds*, *Tootsie*, and *Tequila Sunrise*, and for small-screen programs like *Baretta* and *St. Elsewhere*. He received Oscar nominations for several films, including *The Champ*, *The Fabulous Baker Boys*, *The Firm*, *Havana*, and *Heaven Can Wait*. He also received a Best Original Song nomination for "It Might Be You" from *Tootsie* and he finally received an Oscar statuette for his 1989 score for Robert Redford's film, *The Milagro Beanfield War*.

His heartfelt score for the film *On Golden Pond*, Oscar-nominated in 1981, includes this touching title theme, a tender piano piece that brilliantly enhances the entire film (as you might recall, a generation-gap tearjerker starring Jane and Henry Fonda and Katharine Hepburn).

Amid all his intense productivity, the Colorado-born Grusin found time to take on additional work. He recorded his own albums and served as a bandleader in the '60s. He formed a production team with partner Larry Rosen in the '70s, producing records for Quincy Jones, Carmen McRae, and Sarah Vaughan. That partnership eventually turned into an official record company, GRP, in 1982, and the duo proceeded to scour the globe for talent. Their efforts paid off as GRP blossomed into a multimillion-dollar operation and a premiere jazz/fusion label thanks to signings like George Benson, Chick Corea, Lee Ritenour, and Earl Klugh.

On his own Grusin dabbled in everything from pop music to symphony orchestras. He conducted the successful GRP Big Band, and he recorded and released dozens of his own recordings, 35 of which remain in print today, including *Mountain Dance* (1979) and *Harlequin* (1985).

You will notice tiny crossed-out notes in the music, right before bigger-sized notes. These are *not* mistakes that the composer forgot to erase! They are *grace notes:* played quickly and softly. Not-crossed-out tiny notes are still quick but a little louder. These ornamental notes, whether crossed-out or not, provide pleasant decoration so be sure to leave them all in!

Great things come in threes, or in 3/4. That means each bar or measure contains three quarter notes (or equivalence). *Note:* this is not a heavily accented three-beat. Rather, just give the first beat a whisper more emphasis! Then think: *one* -two- three- It's- e-asy.

Don't muddy up the pond by racing into it. Rather glide softly and steadily like a swan. *Andante rubato* indicates a slow walking speed and strict rhythmic flow. Similarly, don't holler. Keep it soft (*p*) and medium soft (*mp*) with an extra quiet sunset at song's end (*ppp*) leaving just a shimmer.

Rather than pussyfooting around, here's a Where's Waldo-type game, with definitions. Try to find these five valuable terms and symbols within this song:

- L.H. stands for left hand.

- *8vb* means play it one octave lower.

- Glissando *(gliss.)*, refers to a quick glide with the fingernails, using either two fingers (index and middle) or the thumb.

- A serrated line represents a broken chord *(arpeggio)* played bottom to top, fast.

- *Poco animato* tells you to play something a little more animatedly.

Now that you've found them, if you have any questions, either ask someone who looks smart or guess. The probability of getting the right answer is exactly the same!

The Rainbow Connection (page 141)

What "When You Wish Upon a Star" is to Disney, "The Rainbow Connection" is to Jim Henson's Children's Television Workshop, creators of the *Sesame Street* franchise. This song evokes the feel-good ideals and charitable spirit of the Muppets. Interestingly, the lyrics take a jab at the overly optimistic Disney track: "Who said that every wish would be heard and answered/when wished on the morning star? Somebody thought of that/and someone believed it/and look what it's done so far."

Written by Paul Williams and Kenneth Ascher and sung initially by *Sesame Street's* first breakout star, Kermit the Frog, the song debuted in the 1979 film *The Muppet Movie*. Since then, the song has been covered dozens, if not hundreds, of times, by everyone from Willie Nelson, who some mistakenly thought wrote the song, to Justin Timberlake, The Carpenters, and Sarah McLachlan. Kermit's warbly rendition, released in the fall of 1979, reached the Top 40, peaking at #25, staying there for nearly two months.

Ascher and Williams, who wrote the entire score to *The Muppet Movie*, received Academy Award nominations for both the song and the score. Ascher, himself a piano player, songwriter, and composer, plays in the Birdland Big Band. His own version of "The Rainbow Connection" can be heard in the closing credits of the Jennifer Aniston film *The Break-Up*. Williams, who often worked closely with Ascher, is also responsible for lots of great pop music, including the Carpenters' "We've Only Just Begun," Barbra Streisand's "Evergreen," and "An Old Fashioned Love Song," by Three Dog Night. He collaborated with Ascher on the soundtrack to *A Star Is Born* and the hit single "You and Me Against the World."

Bounce over this rainbow. "Moderately, with a lilt" means a peppy 3/4 time. How else would you play a song that ends with "da de da do"?

Bounce to the top of the rainbow (about halfway through) and peek where the key goes higher! That way you'll be ready when the key of A (three sharps) changes to B♭ (two flats).

Look up! The sections with fewer guitar chords above the music are more thoughtful in nature, and you can soften a little. Be ready to hop back in, though, to get that pot of gold!

Raindrops Keep Fallin' on My Head (page 146)

Burt Bacharach scrutinized a scene in George Roy Hill's movie *Butch Cassidy and the Sundance Kid*. He'd been assigned to score the film and he knew he needed something special for a scene in which Paul Newman and Katherine Ross take their unsteady bicycle ride. The song-writer had a phrase in mind, "Raindrops keep falling on my head," a thought that Bacharach felt typified the hi-jinx of the film's main characters. After writing the song based on that line, Bacharach had to talk the producers into running the song at all; that's how unusual it was for the time. After getting the okay, he had to find a singer quickly, a search that ended, reluctantly, with a little-known Texas singer named B.J. Thomas. Nervous and apprehensive, Thomas came out to Los Angeles to cut the track, a trial that took him so long, he ended up being a little hoarse on the version of the song featured in the movie. Exasperated, Bacharach let Thomas rest his vocal cords and he re-cut the song in New York City two weeks later for a version released to radio.

The song proved to be a monster hit. Not only did it win an Academy Award for Best Original Song, it hit the top of the charts and stayed for a full month. Released in 1969, at the peak of Flower Power and hippie culture, acid trips, and psychedelia, "Raindrops Keep Fallin' on My Head," with its simplicity and fresh melody, etched its way into the collective consciousness of a nation, and helped underscore the tremendous success of Hill's film. Thomas even sang it on the next year's television broadcast of The Academy Awards.

Thomas cut one more Bacharach song "Everybody's Out of Town," that only slightly dented the charts. He'd venture on to considerable fame, though, thanks in large part to that right place/right time encounter with a desperate Bacharach in search of a voice.

The rhythm is your umbrella in this easygoing, up-tempo ballad. Remember that dotted notes are a beat plus a half. The overall effect is a skip in your step!

The middle section ("But there's one thing I know. . .") softens the rhythm a little and has a ballad feel. The soft middle of this sweet treat quickly returns to the sturdy outer core.

Get ready. The big ending is signaled by a *fermata* (a dot with a hat). Make sure those final notes are played accented, louder, and with some gusto!

Love Theme from "St. Elmo's Fire" (page 149)

Canadian David Foster, a multiple-Grammy-winning artist, composed the score for the film *St. Elmo's Fire*, which produced two hits, including the stunning instrumental love theme. Over the years Foster has worked with the biggest names in the music biz, names like Celine Dion, Barbra Streisand, Kenny Rogers, George Harrison, Whitney Houston, Michael Jackson, Mariah Carey, Destiny's Child, Vanessa Williams, Anne Murray, and Andrea Bocelli. That's some pretty impressive company!

The achievements continue. Foster composed "Winter Games," the theme song to the 1988 Winter Olympics held in Calgary, Alberta. He also, along with Kenneth "Babyface" Edmonds, wrote "The Power of the Dream" as the official song of the 1996 Summer Olympics. His orchestral, super-cinematic style is superb at creating visual images, which is why his score for *St. Elmo's Fire*, and the love theme in particular, received such high praise. It reached #15 on the *Billboard* hit list as well, becoming that rare commodity: a hit instrumental song.

The other song from the soundtrack that scaled even higher was the chart-topping "St. Elmo's Fire (Man in Motion)," recorded by John Parr. The tune, better known in Canada, was inspired by the Canadian wheelchair activist hero, Rick Hansen, who successfully trekked around the world in a wheelchair to raise awareness of spinal cord issues. The tune and Hansen's cause earned worldwide attention.

So did the movie, which, in retrospect, did an outstanding job of framing the decade of the '80s, from the dialogue and the score to the hairstyles and the fashions. If you're feeling nostalgic about the '80s, then throw this baby on, witness the entanglements of Rob, Demi, Allie, Judd, Emilio, Andrew, and Mare, and let the memory reel roll. Action!

This smooth tune starts moderately softly (*mp*), heats up quickly to relatively loud (*mf*) and keeps a full, wonderful symphonic feel throughout!

Count only two beats per measure! 2/2 is also called *cut time* and is marked by a c with a line through it. Also, take time to study the key signature. This one is in A♭, which has four flats (B♭, E♭, A♭, and D♭). Play the scale a couple of times to burn it into your mind!

Theme from "Schindler's List" *(page 151)*

In contrast to the swashbuckling, space-soaring, boulder-rolling scores of his past, John Williams' work for Steven Spielberg's *Schindler's List* is sad and haunting, subtle in a way that we are unaccustomed to hearing from the composer. There are no big brassy moments, no epic, swelling themes, just dark hints of drama and pinches of melancholy, the equivalent of adding a dash of potent spice to a flavorful stew. Just enough enhances the flavor perfectly. Williams approaches the horrors on screen with a beauty so primordial that the score exudes heartbreak at every harmonic turn. The result, particularly including the heartrending theme, is utterly chilling.

In the nearly three decades that Spielberg has now been transforming the expectations of moviegoers, Williams has been in lockstep with him, taking the evocative pictures on the screen and putting them to music, culminating with the one-two punch in 1993 of *Schindler's List* and *Jurassic Park*. Along the way, they combined for 13 Oscar nominations and three wins for Best Score, making them, unofficially of course, the most successful director/composer tandem in the history of the world!

The *Schindler's List* project actually almost never came to be. When Williams first saw the rough cut of the film, he demurred at the thought of scoring it, thinking it would be too challenging, and out of his league. Spielberg essentially perished the thought, and told Williams to hire world-classic violinist Itzhak Perlman to help him out. In fact, many credit Perlman's performances for making *Schindler's List* as fabulous as it is. With such able-bodied assistance on hand, Williams felt better prepared to break musical ground. And *Schindler's List* remains one of his most spectacular and memorable scores.

Hauntingly beautiful melodies tell this story of adversity and triumph. Play the right hand alone once to hear those guiding voices. Now add the left hand and feel all its beauty.

The first chord and many others in this rich arrangement are *arpeggios* (rolled chords). Stroke those quickly but gently to create an orchestral mood.

Take a moment to note all the timing *(tempo)* and volume *(dynamics)* markings in this passionate piece. It's easy to lose oneself in emotion, so let these guide your expression.

Hold and give a slight accent to notes that have a line or dash (-) above or below them. This is called *tenuto*, from the Italian word *tenere*, which means to hold.

Somewhere in Time *(page 153)*

Is it possible for a soundtrack to be more memorable than the film it scores? Best case, of course, is that the music enhances the film. But with *Somewhere in Time*, the time-travel romance, John Barry becomes the star of the show. And he's the composer!

Director Jeannot Szwarc's 1980 film, featuring Christopher Reeve and Jane Seymour, didn't fare so well upon its release. But over the years it has become a word-of-mouth classic. Much of that groundswell of enthusiasm can be attributed to Barry's swooning, passionate score, which during the title track can be downright intoxicating. With a swirling, string-saturated series of compositions revolving around a classic Rachmaninoff piece, this soundtrack is full of drama, emotion, and beauty. It is one of those rare pieces of music that never grows old. Helping to hold it in place is Rachmaninoff's lovely "Rhapsody on a Theme of Paganini."

John Barry is considered one of the "Big Four" of late 20th century film composers (the others being John Williams, Jerry Goldsmith, and Henry Mancini), and deservedly so. Having scored epic pictures like *Born Free*, *Out of Africa*, and *Dances with Wolves*, he has more than earned his reputation. With *Somewhere in Time* he nails the desperate helplessness of an ill-fated, tragic, but undeniably passionate affair. (You're familiar with those, right?) Like James Cameron's *Titanic* and its score, the music pushes you to fall in love with the film, the characters, and the setting. And while we're on the subject, fans of *Titanic* might be interested to know that *Somewhere in Time* takes place in 1912, the same year our dear massive ship hit the iceberg, blew a gasket (or two), and sank.

Take your time in this moderately slow C major journey. The melody is most certainly the focus here so be sure to let it sing out!

The time signature is 4/4 but not strict! You'll find lots of *quarter note triplets* (three notes played in two beats), plus three note phrases, which produce a fluid, timeless quality.

The left hand is the supporting actor, not the star, so play through that once, solo, to make sure it's solid. Then add the stellar right hand and watch how well they share the stage.

The ending is big, but hold the fireworks! Keep in mind it's a fairly mellow piece, so the accented ending (*ffz*) should be strong, but not quite a cannon blast.

Somewhere, My Love *(page 155)*

Director David Lean and composer Maurice Jarre hit it pretty big with their debut collaboration, *Lawrence of Arabia*, in 1962, so they decided to give it another try a few years later. *Doctor Zhivago* was the result. Not a bad one-two punch, especially considering the first was set in a sunny and sandy locale, while the latter — set in gray and snowy Russia — was quite the opposite.

In the liner notes to the soundtrack, Jarre explains the predicament of scoring *Zhivago*. "I had six weeks to write and record the score for *Doctor Zhivago*, so I was forced to compose many minutes of music each day. Any composer knows that inspiration does not always come when you need it . . . But not working with David Lean. There are rarely problems with inspiration when you are working for a great director."

Indeed, there are few problems to be found with Jarre's score. "Somewhere, My Love," often known as "Lara's Theme," did give him some problems, though. As the story goes, Jarre, quite excited, informed Lean he had a theme he wanted the director to hear. Lean thought Jarre could do better, so he sent him back to the drawing board. The next one, Lean insisted, was too sad. A third attempt proved "too fast." Finally, Lean told Jarre to forget about Russia and forget about the film. He told him to imagine himself in the mountains with his girlfriend. Jarre spent a weekend in the mountains around Los Angeles with his romantic friend, and then, upon his return, took a crack at a fourth theme. Lean heard it and proclaimed, "That's it! That's the one!"

Paul Francis Webster took "Lara's Theme," added lyrics to it, and called it "Somewhere, My Love." It became a massive hit for Ray Conniff and a signature tune for Andy Williams.

When you try this character's theme on piano, you will hear not the echoes of Russia, or the weighty, epic nature of the film, but a simple tribute to love itself; a fresh, light, beautiful melody that will linger in your mind long after the piano strings stop resonating. It remains one of the most recognizable love songs ever written for film.

Move fast, volume-wise! This exotic ballad bounds from soft to moderately loud (*p-mf*) in the first two measures, so don't hesitate.

Accidentals, added sharps and flats, are scattered about like rose petals, so sneak a peek ahead. Don't forget the song's key, G major, also contains F♯ and you'll soon be unlocking this treasure.

Three's company, so be sure to give only two beats to those triplets (marked with a 3). Also be sure not to rush them as they add a wonderful, wandering, and searching feel to this classic.

Somewhere Out There *(page 158)*

Before James Horner wrote the score for *Titanic*, he composed music for several other films, including the beloved animated flick, *An American Tail*, in 1986. Horner collaborated on "Somewhere Out There," the film's breakout tune, with songwriters Barry Mann and Cynthia Weil. In fact, the song is used twice in the film. For its first appearance it's sung by the characters themselves — siblings Fievel and Tanya, voiced by Phillip Glasser and Betsy Cathcart. In the closing credits, a more produced version appears, with Linda Ronstadt and James Ingram handling the vocals.

The closing credits version, of course, is the one that got all the airplay. The single won two Grammy Awards in 1988 for Song of the Year and Best Song for a Motion Picture. It also received a nomination for the Best Original Song Oscar. The Ronstadt-Ingram single went to #2 on the *Billboard* "Hot 100" singles chart in the spring of 1987.

Horner demonstrated a flair for scoring kids' films. He also composed for *Casper*, *Balto*, *The Land Before Time*, and the sequel to *An American Tail*, subtitled *Fievel Goes West*. His work for *Titanic*, though, earned him his real stripes. His soundtrack to the James Cameron film, which starred Leonardo DiCaprio and Kate Winslet, was deeply inspired by the ethereal vibes of Irish vocal group Clannad and sold 24 million copies. But before you assume it's the best-selling soundtrack of all time, think again. It's currently third on the all-time list, behind Whitney Houston's *The Bodyguard* (37 million) soundtrack and the Bee Gees *Saturday Night Fever* (40 million). That's a lotta jive talkin'!

This melodic and rich tune craves expression! The sustain pedal, plus small changes in *dynamics* (volume) and *tempo* (speed), will make this one otherworldly!

Skip forward and check out the fun and interesting adventure. In several sections Horner introduces a bounty of sharps and flats! Enjoy the escapade, because in a blink you're back in the key of C.

Get those repeats right the first time! There are a couple of *codas* (repeats) in this piece. Be ready and you won't flip or lose the mood for the big finale!

Spartacus - Love Theme *(page 163)*

When Stanley Kubrick signed on to direct *Spartacus*, an epic slave-turned-gladiator historical drama that opened in 1960, he was only 30 years old. The producers' plans included a huge budget for the time — $12 million — and a cast of over 10,000, including some of the biggest names in the business: Kirk Douglas, Laurence Olivier, Jean Simmons, and Peter Ustinov. This was a daunting task for someone with relatively little experience. Of course, the egotistical Kubrick certainly proved up to it.

Scoring a film of such sweeping scope fell into the hands of Alex North, an American composer who had previously done the jazzy *A Streetcar Named Desire* and many other important films. North was a modernist composer, meaning he didn't rely on traditional, classical instrumentation of the day for his themes, and his work on *Spartacus* exhibits his modernist tendency, even as he remains true to the historical context of the film. "Love Theme" marks the relationship between Spartacus, played by Kirk Douglas, and Varinia, the slave-girl, for which Jean Simmons received an Academy Award nomination. The "Love Theme" is the film's most accessible excerpt of music. It was sung by Terry Callier, a soulful folksinger from Chicago who released important music in the '60s.

Throughout his career, North tallied an impressive 15 Oscar nominations, though he never came home with the statuette. North and iconic spaghetti western legend Ennio Morricone are the only film composers to receive a Lifetime Achievement Award from the Academy, perhaps as a sort of consolation for never having received the top award. Without question, North deserves the recognition for occupying such a unique place in the development of film music. Prior to North, composers worked almost exclusively in a style held over from the 19th century romantics. With his use of jazz, progressive harmonies, and thematic intensity, North's music heralded a more modern era. His inventive film scores expanded on the potential of the medium and proved "instrumental" in sending film music off in innovative new directions.

This haunting jewel is about melody, so play the melody alone first. Look for slight variations, called *variations on a theme*, a practice common in both jazz and classical music.

Tiptoe in, but saunter out! The opening volume is soft (*p*), quickly increasing to medium soft (*mp*), then growing to medium loud (*mf*) by the end. No sonic boom, though, keep it smooth and gradual!

This tune does not have a typical 3/4 feel. The third beat of the measure (not the first) often gets the accent. So, keep it upbeat.

Speak Softly, Love (Love Theme) *(page 165)*

Back in 1972, *The Godfather* ruled. Not just down in Sicily, but in theaters. It would ultimately be rated as one of the greatest films of all time; currently, it's ranked second behind *Citizen Kane*. On the eve of the Academy Awards, though, there arose a controversy about its soundtrack. Nina Rota, the esteemed Italian composer responsible for the score, was on the list of Academy Award nominees for Best Original Score. But at the last minute someone had noticed that Rota had repurposed the film's theme from a previous movie he had scored called *Fortunella* back almost 15 years earlier. While the two films were very different, the melody of both tunes was indeed the same, so the Academy folks yanked Rota's *Godfather* score from the list of nominees. As an interesting addendum to the story, Rota's score for the film's sequel, *Godfather II*, also earned a nomination for Best Original Score, and actually won. Oddly, that soundtrack also included the very same *Fortunella* theme that excluded the original *Godfather* film from Oscar consideration. Hmmmm.

Rota, the grandson of a famous pianist, grew up a child prodigy on piano. He started writing music at the age of 8 and went on to compose for the stage, ballet, and opera as well as stand-alone concert pieces. But his most memorable and enduring work was done for film, largely because he worked with well-known Italian film directors Frederico Fellini and Franco Zeffirelli. He scored many of Fellini's best-known films: *La Strada*, *La Dolce Vita*, and *The Clowns*, among others. For Zeffirelli, Rota is best remembered for the Shakespeare scores, in particular *Romeo and Juliet*. Rota's Italian origin made him the ideal choice for director Francis Ford Coppola's *Godfather* series.

 Don't let those sweet tones fade. The abundance of held notes is a signature of this classic. Like an accordion player stretching notes, use your fingers and sustain pedal to make those harmonies linger!

Resist melodrama in this dignified and moderately soft (*mp*) piece. The hauntingly beautiful melody is slow and steady in this wonderful drama.

The lyric "Wine-colored days . . ." introduces *triplets* (three notes in one beat) and a slightly different mood. In this bridge section, there's a brief, light-headed reminiscence, but it only lasts a sip or two.

Take My Breath Away (Love Theme) (page 167)

Giorgio Moroder, an Italian award-winning musician and composer, has worn many hats over the years, but the hit-maker chapeau may be the one he most prefers, or at least the one he wears on special occasions. Moroder, along with lyricist Tom Whitlock, wrote "Take My Breath Away," the smash love song from *Top Gun*, performed by the band Berlin. It won the Academy Award for Best Original Song and the Golden Globe for Best Song in 1987.

Moroder, who had hits on his own and as a member of Munich Machine during his career, also ran a successful recording studio in the '80s and '90s called Musicland Studio in Munich, where Elton John and Led Zeppelin, among others, crafted their recordings. He produced records too, having worked with acts like David Bowie, Janet Jackson, Melissa Manchester, Debbie Harry, and, most famously, Donna Summer, whose hit "Love to Love You, Baby" can still be heard on dance floors everywhere in the universe. If that weren't enough, Moroder scored the soundtrack to the hit movie *Midnight Express*, and won his first Academy Award for Best Film Score in the year of its release, 1978. Moroder also went on to score other very popular films such as *American Gigolo*, *Flashdance* (Irene Cara's "Flashdance . . . What a Feeling" earned an Academy Award, too), *Cat People*, and *Scarface*. *Scarface*, in particular, has experienced a resurgence of popularity due to its usage in the massively popular video game franchise "Grand Theft Auto."

Much of Moroder's reputation came because of his pioneering work on synthesizer-based sound. He first discovered Moog synthesis at the start of the '70s and he could be found at the cutting edge of electronic music-making ever since. Yet while he established a trademark techno sound in the pop arena with his many dance and pop hits, he managed to retain a more diverse and sophisticated balance through his soundtrack work. Today, Moroder's name can be read somewhere in the credits of over 200 gold and platinum albums.

This memorable hook grabs you immediately! The first notes introduce the theme in a manner loud (moderately) and proud. Also, don't forget to strongly accent the steady 4/4 timing that serves as the heartbeat (and breath) of this hit.

 Four flats mean you're in the key of A♭. Find those flatted notes on the piano: B♭, E♭, A♭, and D♭. Now find the *natural* (non-flatted) notes: C, F, and G. Close your eyes and engrave them in your memory, take a deep breath, and you're good to go!

The repeat and fade ending may not be right for every audience. To be ready for that scenario, find the song's key (here: A♭) and search the music for a lovely, full A♭ chord. Then, when your fans lean forward at the end, waiting to applaud, let it ring!

Theme from "Terms of Endearment" *(page 175)*

Born March 5, 1951, in New York City, composer Michael Gore is, among other notable facts, the brother of singer/songwriter Leslie Gore, the same Leslie Gore responsible for hits like "It's My Party" and "You Don't Own Me" back in the early '60s.

Initially, Michael followed in his sister's footsteps as a songwriter. Later he joined Columbia as a staff writer, moving into producing classical recordings before embarking on a career as a soundtrack composer. His work for the 1980 flick *Fame* kicked his film-scoring career off with a bang. He earned Academy Awards for both Best Score and Best Song ("Fame"). He followed that early triumph with another: His work for James Brooks' film *Terms of Endearment*, the 1983 tearjerker starring Debra Winger, Jack Nicholson, and Shirley MacLaine. And he followed that up with the massively musical hit *Footloose*, starring Kevin Bacon.

Throughout his career, Gore demonstrated that not only could he score effectively, he could also pull a hit or two out of his pocket when the need arose. He did so first with the aforementioned "Fame," then again with 1993's "Still It's You" from the film *Mr. Wonderful*, written with lyricist Dean Pitchford.

But back to his work on *Terms*. Gore's main theme is the one that sticks, and the one used to most effectively hammer home Brooks' emotional points. Unfortunately, Gore's work on *Terms* wasn't recognized with an Oscar, eclipsed on Oscar night by Bill Conti's work on *The Right Stuff* (Tom Hanks) that took home the statue.

Classic! Remember when songs started *soft*, got *loud*, then *soft* again? Well, those days are back. *Dynamics* (volume) here run the gamut, starting soft (*p*), gradually building to very loud (*ff*) and ending with a hush. Show range by adhering to this arc crafted to express the depth and breadth of life's most cherished gift: relationships.

There'll be no awkward pauses in this melodious conversation with proper use of the *sustain pedal*. That pedal (which is located on the far right) lets the notes ring out. The melody here starts single-note but later expands to become part of a chord (at measure 17). So, your pinkie finger will then be plunking the melody up at the top. The pedal can soften and smooth the flow. Play it a few times there, releasing the pedal regularly, so it blends, not blurs, steady as an easy breeze blowing.

Staff alert: Bars/measures 5, 6, 9, and 10 use a dual treble clef. Both staves (plural for *staff*, which is the five lines that hold the notes) use it. Typically, there's a bass clef down there. So be ready for this event with all staff on deck!

Dots and *sims* here refer to *staccato* playing style, not computer stuff. A dot above or below a note or chord means play the note(s) quickly with no sustain. Think pop, pop, pop, pop. The term *sim.* just means *similarly*, so continue that style *(staccato)* until that pattern ends. Turn the computer off for at least three or four minutes while you play this gem!

A Time for Us (Love Theme) *(page 172)*

Okay, so let's try to get this straight. Nina Rota penned a song, let's call it the "Love Theme from Romeo and Juliet," for Franco Zeffirelli's film of roughly the same name. But there are four different sets of lyrics written for the song. The film's version of the song is called "What Is a Youth," and features words by Eugene Walter. Another version of the song, called "A Time for Us," featuring lyrics by Larry Kusik and Eddie Snyder, fell into the hands of Henry Mancini, whose own version topped the American pop charts in 1969. And, finally, an Italian reworking of the song, called "Ai Giocchi Addio," is written in Italian and often performed by opera singers, while Josh Groban worked out a version of his own, which is still another Italian translation of the American adaptation, "Un Giorno Per Noi." Those lyrics were written by Elsa Morante. Got that?

The bottom line is that Rota wrote brilliant music, the kind with which the universe could identify. In the film, the theme is used twice principally, once wispily and effeminately at the masque, and again with the full-bodied stringed version later in the score. Either way, it's hard to watch the film without allowing Rota's score to whisk you away. Yet, although the love theme is the centerpiece of the score, much of Rota's music has a more period sound, and is less overtly romantic. The character themes for *Romeo and Juliet* are simple and fairly modest, utilizing basic strings and woodwind solos. But when the love theme appears, Rota opts for a less modest orchestral presence. Even then, he restrains from overly indulgent readings until near the end, allowing it to unfold with dramatic emotional resonance. Such a tragic result deserves a bang as big as all that, wouldn't you agree?

It's well worth your time to decide the *fingering patterns* (which fingers play which notes) early and then stick to it!

Avoid the urge to speed up as you progress. If you remember to keep it slow and expressive you won't lose your groove come performance time!

Make the melody soar! Despite the minor key (G minor) voicing, this sweet and beautiful melody brings hope and inspiration to lovers of all ages.

Unchained Melody (page 181)

Lyricist Hy Zaret is the man responsible for writing the compelling words to "Unchained Melody," one of the most frequently recorded songs of the 20th century. Zaret died in 2007, a month shy of his 100th birthday, but his song will undoubtedly live on for many years to come. To date, it has been officially recorded more than 300 times, according to the American Society of Composers, Authors and Publishers, which listed it as one of the 25 most-performed musical works of the 20th century.

The song originally appeared in 1955 for a film called *Unchained*, which was about a convict torn between finishing out his sentence and escaping the confines of prison to return to his wife and family. Interestingly, Zaret refused the producer's request to work the word "unchained" into the lyrics, instead writing to express the feelings of a lover who has "hungered for your touch a long, lonely time."

While the film itself didn't make much of an impact, it did bring Zaret and composer Alex North an Academy Award nomination for Best Song. As a post-script, few associate Zaret and North with the song, which has been recorded by artists as diverse as Elvis Presley, Lena Horne, U2, Guy Lombardo, Vito & The Salutations, and Joni Mitchell. An instrumental version was a #1 hit in 1955 for Les Baxter, while a vocal version by Al Hibbler reached #3 the same year. But most remember the song from The Righteous Brothers' version. That recording, produced by Phil Spector, reached #4 on the *Billboard* chart in 1965, and hit again 25 years later with its major presence in the *Ghost* soundtrack, again without crediting North. Then again, North is no stranger to being left out of things. In 1968, when he was contracted to compose the score to Stanley Kubrick's masterpiece *2001: A Space Odyssey*, he did so, creating a sweeping, fully symphonic work. But the irascible Kubrick rejected North's submission and replaced it with standard classical fare by traditional composers. North's unused score for the film came out only in the early '90s, after North's death, overseen by his good friend, another extraordinary composer, Jerry Goldsmith (*Alien*, *Legend*, *Mulan*).

Unchaining this great melody takes some extra notes. But don't worry, the 12/8 time signature doesn't mean you have to count to 12. Instead, count four groups of three. Easy as one-two-three . . . times four, that is!

If this song sounds like a cat running on the piano, you missed the two treble clefs at the beginning. That just means you read it like playing two right hands.

The rolling feel gets rocking by the end. The last verse gets gradually louder (*crescendo* or *cresc.*) and ends big with an accented double *fortissimo* (very loud). Be sure to slow the end (*molto rit.*) so we don't miss those fireworks!

The right hand crosses the left hand in the eighth measure. A trial run of this neat trick will keep your hands unchained for some fancy finger work!

Up Where We Belong (page 191)

A few ironies exist in the back stories of "Up Where We Belong," the #1 hit and award-winning song from the 1982 military love story *An Officer and a Gentleman*. The song, written by Jack Nitzsche and Buffy Sainte-Marie, with lyrics by Will Jennings, was originally performed by the duet of English rock singer Joe Cocker and pop star Jennifer Warnes. Nitzsche and Sainte-Marie, who were married at the time, were something of an eccentric couple. Nitzsche produced many famous recordings and worked with many legends during his career, from Sonny Bono and Buffalo Springfield to Tom Petty and the Rolling Stones. His unconventional work with Phil Spector on records by The Ronettes, The Crystals, and Ike and Tina Turner was legendary, likewise was his psychedelic work on The Monkees' soundtrack *Head*. Sainte-Marie, a Native-American singer/songwriter, was a topical, politically-charged artist and an integral force in the "Red Power" movement. She vehemently criticized the United States government and its treatment of her Native American people, even going so far as to claim the American government had blacklisted her. That the two of these talents found each other — they married in 1983 — and managed to write such a hugely popular theme in such a mainstream movie with stars like Richard Gere and Debra Winger seems to run contrary to their beliefs, or at least their senses of creative aesthetics.

Then again, they took the jackpot from their seemingly ironic contribution to the bank. Not only did it hit the top spot on the charts, it remained there for three weeks and won the Academy Award and Golden Globe for Best Original Song in 1983. Cocker and Warnes also earned a trophy, from the Grammys, for Best Pop Performance by a Duo or Group.

Nitzsche produced other very successful soundtracks, including *Stand by Me*, *9 1/2 Weeks*, and the Oscar-nominated *One Flew Over the Cuckoo's Nest*.

An all-important pause in the vocal melody comes right before the classic refrain, "Love, lift us up . . ." That vocal rest puts an accent on the second beat, on the word "love." This pop music technique gets folks moving (a sense of rocking and rolling, if you will . . .).

Get down a little (volume-wise) following the first refrain. Find the marking (*dim.* or *diminuendo*) just before the repeat. Relax your fingers a little and save the heavy lifting for the end!

This soulful classic goes one key up to the mountaintop. Preview the key change that happens in the second verse (from D to E♭). You'll recognize it because the sharps change to flats on the staff. Then let your inner eagle fly!

Either stay up where you belong or head down the mountain. It's your choice with the optional ending. Repeat and fade, or let some sweet, soulful jazz chords take you home!

The Way We Were (page 188)

Another example of a song that, arguably, eclipses the film from which it stems, "The Way We Were" ranks high on the list of the greatest movie tunes of all time. On the American Film Institute's Top 100 film songs, it appears at #8. The Academy Award people sealed its fate with statuettes for Best Original Dramatic Score and Best Original Song.

Composed by Marvin Hamlisch with lyrics by Alan and Marilyn Bergman, the song dominated radio in 1973 and 1974, charting for nearly six months and climbing to #1 for almost a month. Hamlisch, whose first job with Streisand was as a rehearsal pianist for *Funny Girl*, has an interesting story. The prestigious Juilliard School accepted him a few months before he turned 7, and he became the youngest person ever to be admitted. The '70s featured his greatest success. He adapted Scott Joplin's ragtime music, and the smash song "The Entertainer," for the Paul Newman/Robert Redford film *The Sting* in 1973. The next year, he cleaned up with the aforementioned two Academy Awards and four Grammys for "The Way We Were." Hamlisch also composed the score to the immensely popular, award-winning Broadway musical *A Chorus Line*. In 1977 he hit it big again with "Nobody Does It Better," a song in the Bond film *The Spy Who Loved Me*, co-written with girlfriend Carole Bayer-Sager and performed by Carly Simon.

Taking all this into account, Hamlisch made good on his original promise as a Juilliard prodigy. (Only anxiety issues and stage fright prohibited him from being a performing act himself.) In fact, Hamlisch is only the second person on the entire planet to have won an Emmy®, a Grammy, a Tony, an Oscar, and a Pulitzer in a single lifetime. The other is Richard Rodgers, of the famed duo Rodgers and Hammerstein.

Keep the opening simple, without lots of emotion. That same repeating theme returns at the end, closing the cover of this scrapbook.

The section beginning "Can it be . . ." welcomes a bit of emotion. Marvin Hamlisch begins preparing us for the grand ending, but be sure to hold back on the sentimental "would we."

Know the ending. There's a dramatic pause before the last two measures, marked by a *caesura* (*//*, which indicates a pause). After that, slow down (*rit.*), roll the chord (*arpeggio*) and remember to top it all off with an accent!

When I Fall in Love (page 195)

Victor Young composed the score to *One Minute to Zero*, a 1952 wartime romance starring Robert Mitchum and Ann Blyth that contains "When I Fall in Love." When the song debuted in the film, it signaled just the beginning for what would soon become a standard, popularized by scores of singers, from Doris Day (1952) and Nat King Cole (1956) to Kenny Rogers and Celine Dion (1993). It was also featured in the recent films *Eyes Wide Shut* and *Sleepless in Seattle*.

Young, a child prodigy on violin and a big band leader later on, wrote scores for more than 350 films including *For Whom the Bell Tolls*, *The Uninvited*, *Samson and Delilah*, *The Greatest Show on Earth*, and *Around the World in Eighty Days*, for which he earned the 1956 Academy Award for Best Score.

Young wrote the song with Edward Heyman, a successful Tin Pan Alley lyricist who collaborated with a variety of composers for works on both Broadway and the silver screen. "Tin Pan Alley" was the nickname given to the street where many music publishers worked during the period of 1880 to 1953, just prior to the dawn of rock 'n' roll. In the late 19th century, New York had become the epicenter of songwriting and music publishing, and publishers converged on the block of West 28th Street between Broadway and Sixth Avenue in Manhattan. As the story goes, a reporter covering the beat of sheet music publishing in New York was walking through the neighborhood and, after hearing the sounds of all the competing pianos emanating from open windows, he wrote that it sounded like a bunch of "tin pans clanging."

When Elvis came along, a song's performance, not its publication or how many copies of sheet music it sold, grew exponentially in importance, while the role of Tin Pan Alley and its creative minds phased out. Still, while it lasted, the collaboration between publishers, songwriters, and songwriting teams created the most important and enduring music in American history, and Tin Pan Alley remains synonymous with the most fruitful period in popular music.

Make a first impression that lasts. Use the sustain pedal immediately to make those climbing left-hand patterns sound linked and smooth *(legato)!*

Live it up! But follow directions too. Play the first verse freely, as marked, followed by the second verse steadily, with feeling. Don't worry, that free feeling returns at the end!

Timing is everything in love and love songs. Although the 4/4 time signature opens (and closes) the tune, the middle part is 12/8 time, which lengthens the phrases. Note that 12 beats are counted in four groups of three!

The final verse jumps a whole step higher. So hop over there and peruse the change from C major to D major. It's easy to find, just look where sharps (♯) appear on the staff lines!

Yellow Submarine *(page 205)*

In the 1968 animated film, *Yellow Submarine,* The Beatles have been recruited by Captain Fred to save Pepperland from the happiness- and music-hating Blue Meanies. In creating the ambience and setting for the film, animator Hans Edelmann and director George Dunning conjured up an odyssey in the very whimsical style of Lewis Carroll's *Alice in Wonderland.* Their tale starts with Captain Fred, lucky enough to escape certain doom by hopping aboard the Yellow Sub. He needs help to save Pepperland, and the intrepid Beatles are more than willing to oblige.

The soundtrack of the film was The Beatles' tenth official album, though The Beatles themselves never really considered it an official entry in their canon. The song of the same name, written mainly by Paul McCartney in 1966, sold over a million copies in just four weeks, earning the band their 21st gold record, a number that vaulted them past Elvis in that category. Only John Lennon's controversial remark that The Beatles were "bigger than Jesus" kept the song from the top of the charts. (The Supremes' "You Can't Hurry Love" also prevented the song from reaching #1.)

The Beatles decided to use Ringo Starr to sing lead vocals on "Yellow Submarine," a ploy the band resorted to whenever the song had light-hearted material ("Octopus's Garden" and "Act Naturally"). The band felt Ringo's voice and Paul's short, easy-to-understand words would be naturally appealing to kids, which many say was Paul's intended audience for "Yellow Submarine." Ringo would get another chance to communicate directly with kids when he undertook a role on the U.K. cartoon *Thomas the Tank Engine,* as the Narrator and Mr. Conductor.

And what about that friendly, partying chorus? Rumor has it that the voices consisted of the studio crew, as well as friends Mal Evans, Neil Aspinall, producer George Martin, Pattie Boyd/Harrison, and the folksinger known as Donovan, McCartney's friend and neighbor at the time, who helped McCartney with uncredited lyric contributions.

The Beatles choose a march tempo here (only The Beatles march in a yellow submarine). All four beats are accented almost equally.

The rhythm is gonna get ya (where the lyric starts, "So we sailed ... "). The sung (and held) introduction ends there and the music becomes rhythmic. Watch for lots of fills (between the melody). They sound like marching band drum rolls!

That loud color is a hint. This yellow submarine is boisterously loud (*f*) at the chorus: "We all live . . . " The rest of the voyage stays moderately loud (*mf*) to remind us it's still rock 'n' roll!

At the lyric "The band begins to play . . . ," have the band ready! Run through the playful triplets (three notes crammed into one beat). Don't worry about room. The pace is slow and it's a big submarine!

You Must Love Me (page 202)

The partnership of lyricist Tim Rice and composer Andrew Lloyd Webber produced a handful of incredibly successful projects, including *Joseph and the Amazing Technicolor Dream Coat* (1968), *Jesus Christ Superstar* (1970), and *Evita* (1976; 1979 in the U.S.). Lloyd Webber would also go on to produce dramatic spectacles such as *Cats* (1981) and *Phantom of the Opera* (1986).

Evita is a musical based on the life of Eva Peron, the former first lady of Argentina. Lloyd Webber and Rice's collaboration first appeared as a concept album, featuring Julie Covington singing the main character's part. From that album, "Don't Cry for Me Argentina" became a hit single and its success on the airwaves gave the stage version of the play a significant boost when it premiered. *Evita* ran for ten years in London's West End theater district. It enjoyed a run of 1568 performances on Broadway before closing there in the summer of 1983.

"You Must Love Me" was not written for the original stage version of the play. Lloyd Webber and Rice tacked it on for the film version, which came out in 1996. It was one of two new songs written for the movie, the other being "She Is a Diamond." It was the first new material from the team of Rice and Lloyd Webber after a 13-year hiatus. "You Must Love Me," performed by Madonna, won an Academy Award and a Golden Globe for Best Original Song from a Motion Picture back in 1997. After several stellar performances by other actresses playing Eva Peron in the stage versions, Madonna owned the part with her own brilliant turn on celluloid. She won a Golden Globe for Best Actress and the film raked in nearly $150 million at the box office worldwide.

We all must go with the flow in this amazing love song. "Flowingly" means to vary the speed *(tempo)* and volume *(dynamics)*, a bit, as you wish.

Be sure to keep it on the slow, soft side but let this beautiful, expressive music be your guide. The lack of tempo or dynamic markings means it's okay to trust yourself on this one!

Colla voce means follow the voice. But whose voice? The singer's, of course! If you're not playing with a singer, ignore this! If you are accompanying a singer then, as you would in love, stick with them!

Look for slightly different music at "Deep in my heart . . ." Ch-ch-changes take place there: *triplets* (three notes in two beats), a bit more rhythmic intensity, and a slowing down *(rit.)* at "frightened you might slip away . . . " But fear not! This must-hear familiar theme quickly returns with a passion!

The Man From Snowy River (Main Title Theme)

from THE MAN FROM SNOWY RIVER
By Bruce Rowland

Moderately

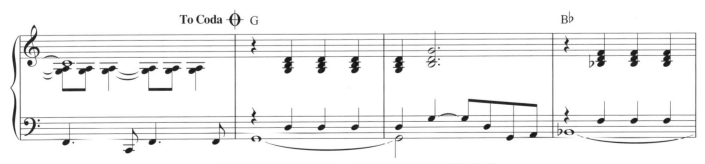

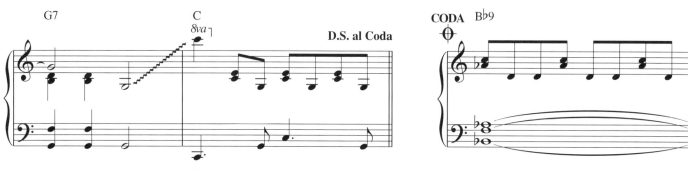

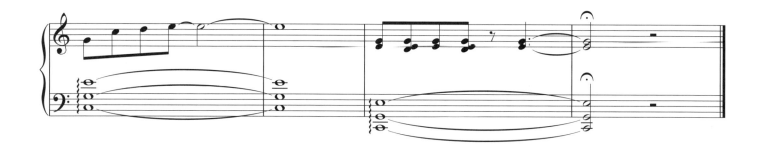

Mission: Impossible Theme

from the Paramount Motion Picture MISSION: IMPOSSIBLE
By Lalo Schifrin

Moderately, with drive

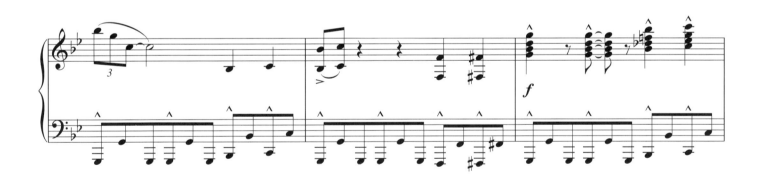

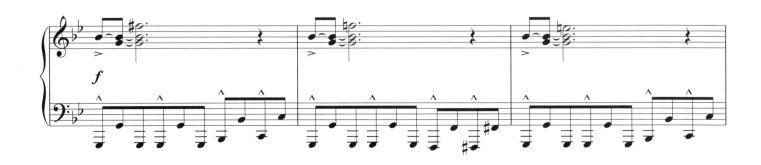

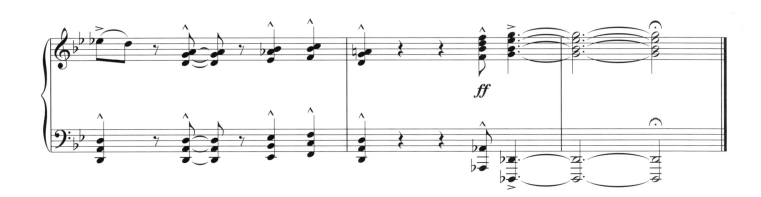

Moon River

from the Paramount Picture BREAKFAST AT TIFFANY'S
Words by Johnny Mercer
Music by Henry Mancini

On Golden Pond

Main Theme from ON GOLDEN POND
Music by Dave Grusin

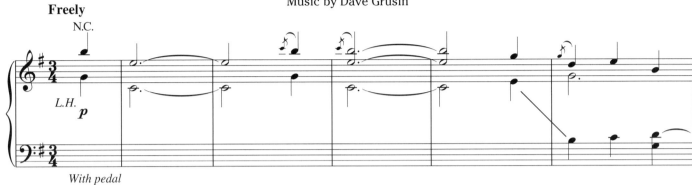

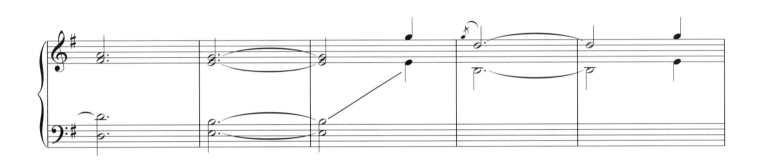

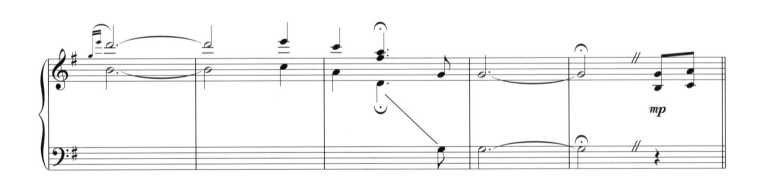

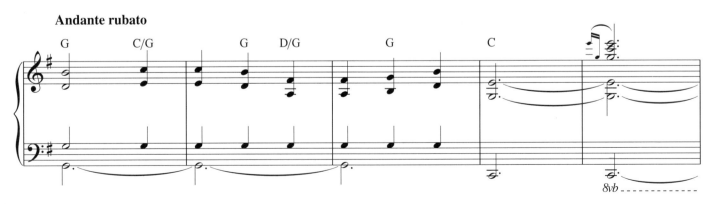

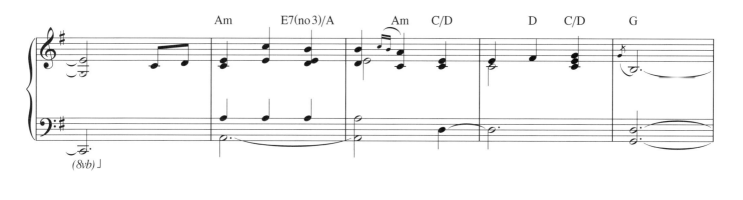

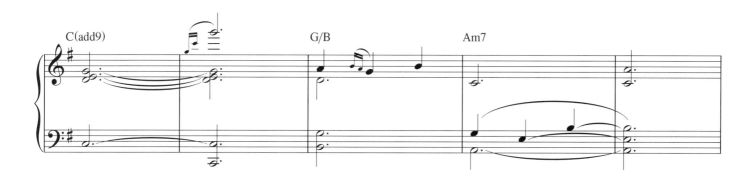

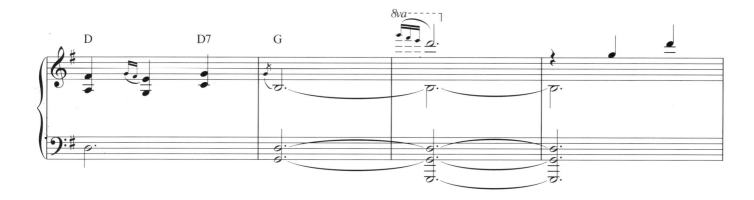

The Music Of Goodbye

from OUT OF AFRICA
Words and Music by John Barry, Alan Bergman and Marilyn Bergman

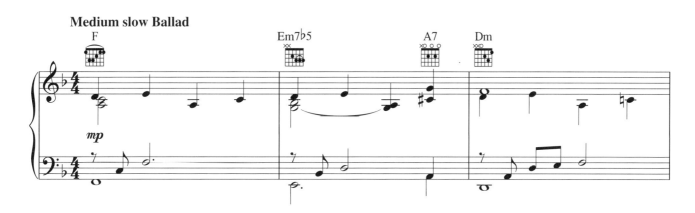

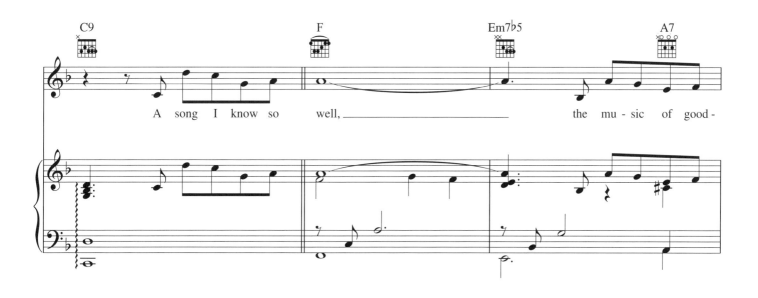

A song I know so well, _____ the mu-sic of good-

bye a - gain. _____ It's there each time we say "Hel - lo." _____

My Heart Will Go On (Love Theme From 'Titanic')

from the Paramount and Twentieth Century Fox Motion Picture TITANIC

Music by James Horner
Lyric by Will Jennings

The Rainbow Connection

from THE MUPPET MOVIE
Words and Music by Paul Williams and Kenneth L. Ascher

Raindrops Keep Fallin' On My Head

from BUTCH CASSIDY AND THE SUNDANCE KID
Lyric by Hal David
Music by Burt Bacharach

Love Theme From "St. Elmo's Fire"

from the Motion Picture ST. ELMO'S FIRE
Words and Music by David Foster

Theme From "Schindler's List"

from the Universal Motion Picture SCHINDLER'S LIST
Music by John Williams

Somewhere In Time

from SOMEWHERE IN TIME
By John Barry

Moderately slow

Somewhere, My Love

Lara's Theme from DOCTOR ZHIVAGO
Lyric by Paul Francis Webster
Music by Maurice Jarre

Moderately, with expression

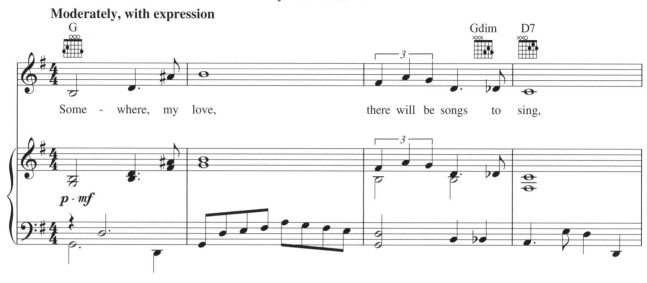

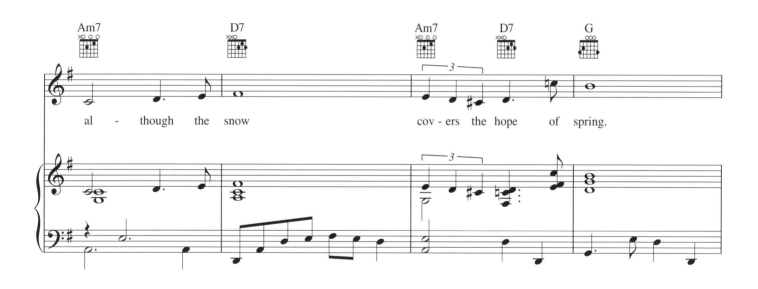

Somewhere Out There

from AN AMERICAN TAIL
Music by Barry Mann and James Horner
Lyric by Cynthia Weil

Spartacus - Love Theme

from the Universal-International Picture Release SPARTACUS
By Alex North

Moderato

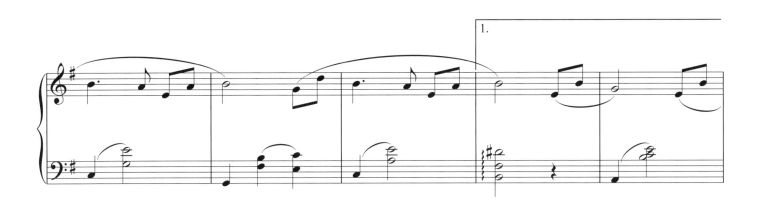

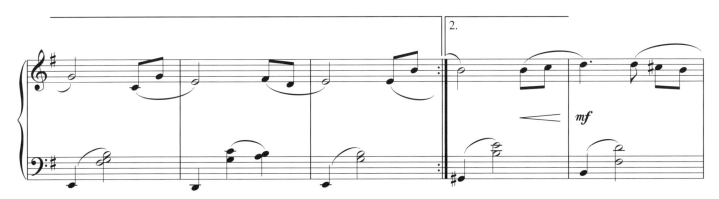

Speak Softly, Love (Love Theme)

from the Paramount Picture THE GODFATHER
Words by Larry Kusik
Music by Nino Rota

Take My Breath Away (Love Theme)

from the Paramount Picture TOP GUN
Words and Music by Giorgio Moroder and Tom Whitlock

Moderately slow

A Time For Us (Love Theme)

from the Paramount Picture ROMEO AND JULIET
Words by Larry Kusik and Eddie Snyder
Music by Nino Rota

Theme From "Terms Of Endearment"

from the Paramount Picture TERMS OF ENDEARMENT
By Michael Gore

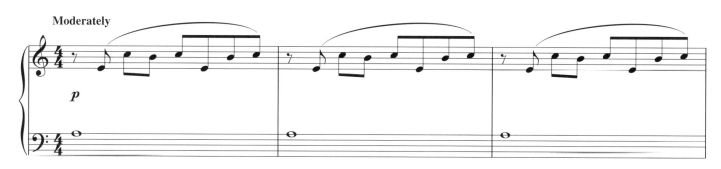

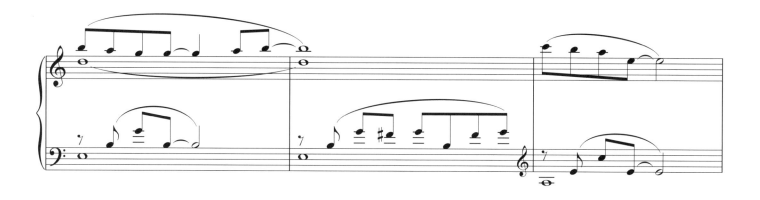

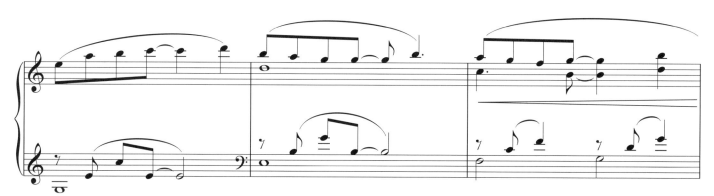

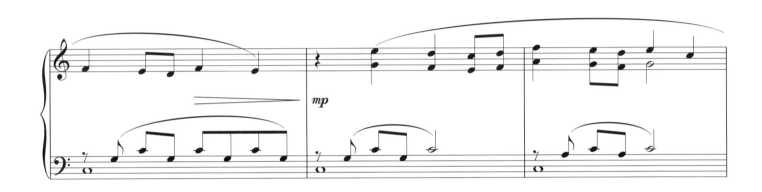

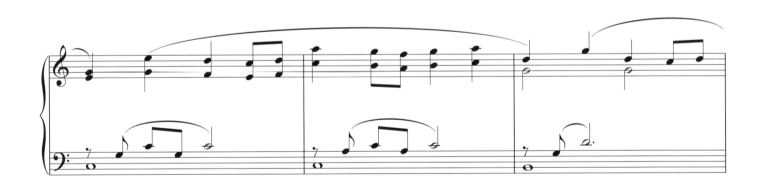

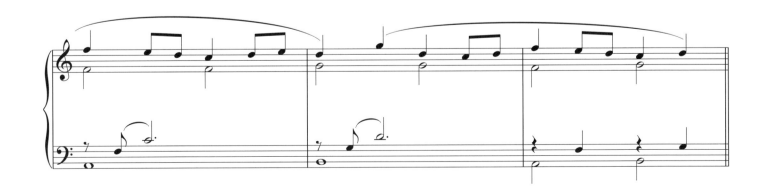

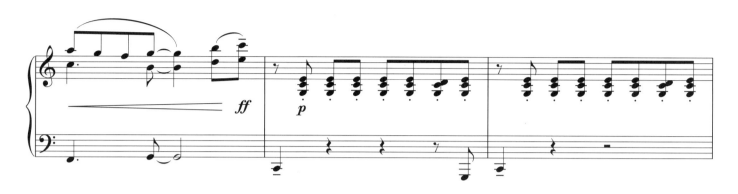

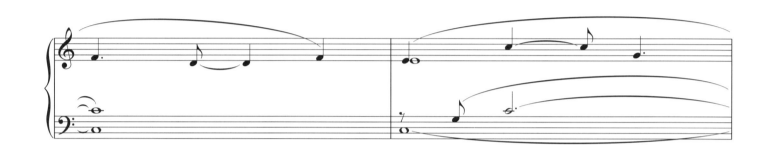

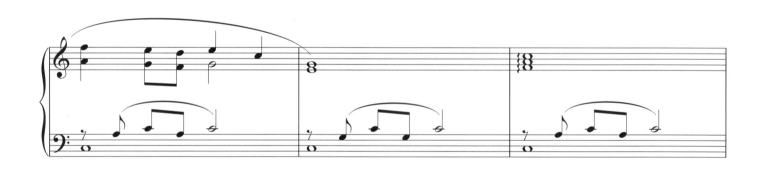

Unchained Melody

from the Motion Picture UNCHAINED
featured in the Motion Picture GHOST
Lyric by Hy Zaret
Music by Alex North

Lone - ly___ riv - ers flow   to   the   sea,   to   the   sea,

to   the ___ o - pen arms _____ of   the   sea, _____ yeah. _____

Lone - ly___ riv - ers sigh,   "Wait for   me, _____ wait for   me.

The Way We Were

from the Motion Picture THE WAY WE WERE
Words by Alan and Marilyn Bergman
Music by Marvin Hamlisch

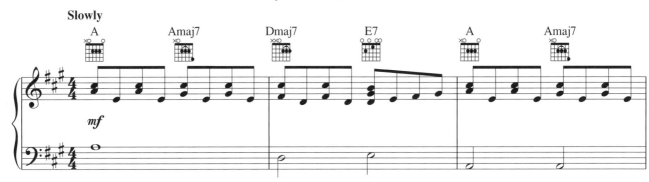

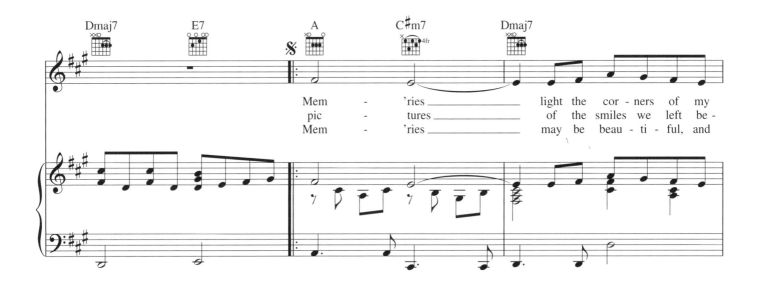

Mem - 'ries _____ light the cor - ners of my
pic - tures _____ of the smiles we left be-
Mem - 'ries _____ may be beau - ti - ful, and

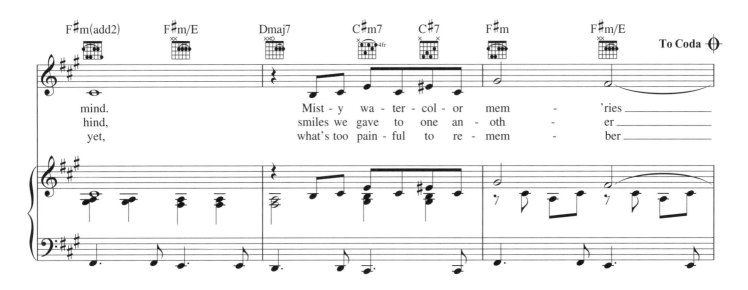

mind.
hind,
yet,

Mist - y wa - ter - col - or mem - 'ries _____
smiles we gave to one an - oth - er _____
what's too pain - ful to re - mem - ber _____

Up Where We Belong

from the Paramount Picture AN OFFICER AND A GENTLEMAN
Words by Will Jennings
Music by Buffy Sainte-Marie and Jack Nitzsche

When I Fall In Love

featured in the TriStar Motion Picture SLEEPLESS IN SEATTLE
from ONE MINUTE TO ZERO
Words by Edward Heyman
Music by Victor Young

You Must Love Me

from the Cinergi Motion Picture EVITA
Words by Tim Rice
Music by Andrew Lloyd Webber

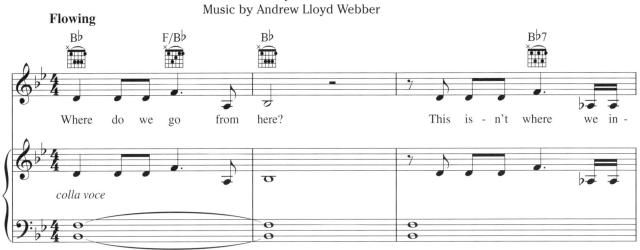

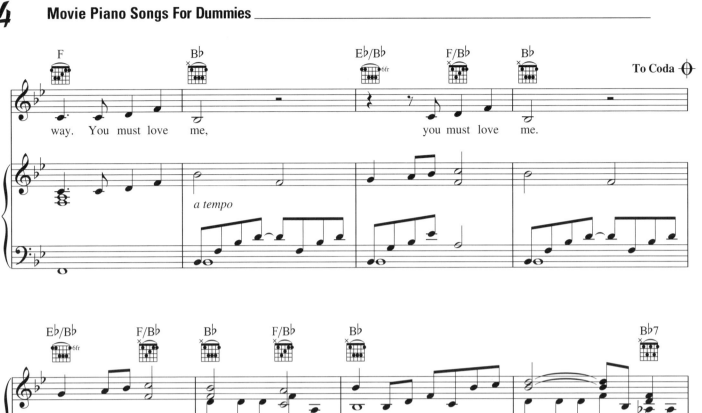

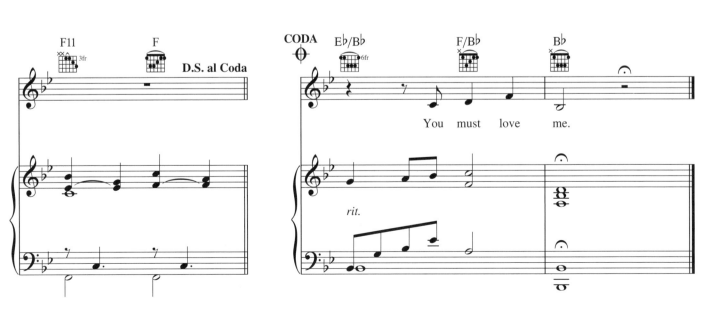

Yellow Submarine

from YELLOW SUBMARINE
Words and Music by John Lennon and Paul McCartney

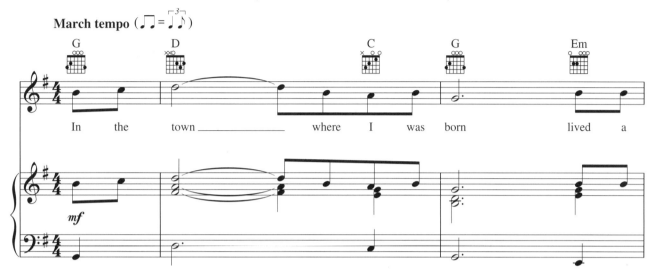

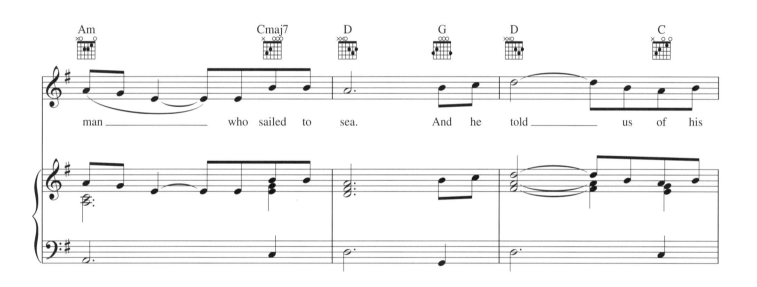